COMING TO
AMERICA

The Hmong

Other Books in the Coming to America series:

The Arabs

The Chinese

The Cubans

The East Indians

The Filipinos

The Germans

The Irish

The Italians

The Jews

The Mexicans

The Vietnamese

COMING TO AMERICA

The Hmong

Kaarin Alisa, Book Editor

GREENHAVEN PRESS

An imprint of Thomson Gale, a part of The Thomson Corporation

THOMSON

GALE

Detroit • New York • San Francisco • New Haven, Conn. • Waterville, Maine • London

Christine Nasso, *Publisher*
Elizabeth Des Chenes, *Managing Editor*

© 2007 Thomson Gale, a part of The Thomson Corporation.

Thomson and Star logo are trademarks and Gale and Greenhaven Press are registered trademarks used herein under license.

For more information, contact:
Greenhaven Press
27500 Drake Rd.
Farmington Hills, MI 48331-3535
Or you can visit our Internet site at http://www.gale.com

Articles in Greenhaven Press anthologies are often edited for length to meet page require-ments. In addition, original titles of these works are changed to clearly present the main thesis and to explicitly indicate the author's opinion. Every effort is made to ensure that Greenhaven Press accurately reflects the original intent of the authors. Every effort has been made to trace the owners of copyrighted material.

Cover photograph reproduced by permission of Darren Hauck/Getty Images.

ISBN-13: 978-0-7377-3500-0
ISBN-10: 0-7377-3500-7

Library of Congress Control Number: 2006938249

Printed in the United States of America
10 9 8 7 6 5 4 3 2 1

973.0495
Hmong

Contents

Foreword   11

Introduction   14

Chapter 1: At War in Laos

1. The Secret U.S. Pact with the Hmong in Laos   24
   Amoun Vang Sayaovong
   An American Hmong immigrant describes an important
   speech given by William Colby, former head of the Central Intelligence Agency. He details Colby's firsthand account of the beginning of the war in Laos and the
   Hmong's ill-fated participation in that covert war.

2. The Hmong Flee Laos   33
   Gary Yia Lee
   A respected Hmong researcher and author describes the
   end of the Laotian war, the immigration of the Hmong
   refugees to other countries, and the continued persecution of the Hmong in Laos.

3. The Great Betrayal of the Hmong   38
   Anthony C. LoBaido
   The original agreement between the United States and
   the Hmong provided that the United States would take
   care of the Hmong that fought with America against the
   Communists. That agreement was broken, ultimately
   leading to the policy of deadly forced repatriation of the
   Hmong back into Laos.

Chapter 2: The Hmong Arrive in America

1. Hmong Refugees Have Difficulty Assimilating   48
   Suzanne C. Dirks
   Many cultural differences have created challenges for the
   first generation of Hmong living in America, including
   cultural beliefs, education, language, and employment.

2. The Hmong Face Barriers to Getting Jobs   **55**
Thomas Moore and Vicky Selkowe

The first wave of Hmong refugees to America is very dependent on public assistance. Research findings show the reasons for this dependence and what the barriers are to independent employment.

3. Growing Old as a Hmong in America   **61**
Kao-Ly Yang

A first-generation Hmong woman who has worked with many elderly Hmong in Wisconsin and California describes how the traditional expectations of first-generation Hmong influence how they want to live in their new home of America.

4. Shamans in the Hmong American Community   **68**
Deborah G. Helsel, Marilyn Mochel,
and Robert Bauer

Substantial differences between the Hmong traditional shaman approach to healing and the American medical approach to healing creates extensive challenges for Western doctors providing care to the Hmong people.

5. Many Hmong Reject Western Psychiatry   **77**
Kaomi Goetz

The Hmong have a strong belief that all illness begins in the soul, and therefore all healing is done at the soul level. This approach to healing creates barriers to the Hmong receiving mental health care for such things as depression and post-traumatic stress disorder.

6. The Hmongs' Success in Minnesota   **81**
Stephen Magagnini

All Hmong refugee communities have had a hard time assimilating in America, but the Hmong in Wisconsin have been more successful than those in California. The reason may be found in the social structure of the communities.

7. Hmong Farm Enterprises in America   **92**
Spencer Sherman

A bold program called the Hiawatha Valley Farm Project helps the Hmong refugees reeducate to Western farming. Instead of traditional slash-and-burn techniques that are illegal in the United States, Western farming techniques are bringing independence back to some Hmong in America.

8. New Hmong Refugees Arrive from Thailand   **102**
Toni Randolph

The first wave of immigrants had few if any skills to apply to life in America. This newest wave of immigrants from Thailand, however, have many skills gained in the refugee camps and have an established Hmong community to get help from when they arrive.

Chapter 3: Hmong Youth Settle into American Culture

1. Hmong Women's Lives Change in America   **107**
Nancy D. Donnelly

There are substantial differences between modern American views and the traditional Hmong views of gender roles. These differences are causing drastic changes in the traditional Hmong familial roles. Hmong women in America are making more money, rejecting arranged marriages, and accepting concepts such as divorce.

2. The Problem of Hmong Gangs   **120**
Brendan McGarvey

A small segment of second-generation Hmong are establishing gangs heavily armed and active in the drug trade, gambling, and prostitution. Because of their fierce warrior reputation, Hmong youth are also being recruited by established gangs in America such as the Bloods and the Crypts.

3. Breaking Away from Tradition   **124**
Christopher Loke

A second-generation Hmong recounts his decision to leave his family and strike out on his own in America, because the traditions of his parents were not ones he wanted to embrace.

4. Hmong Children Turn to the Courts for Help   **130**

Brian Bonner

Hmong youth in America, especially female, are becoming dissatisfied with the traditional Hmong leadership's way of handling domestic disputes. They are increasingly turning to the police and the American court system to help them out of abusive situations.

5. Young Hmong Musicians   **135**

Nzong Xiong

Hmong youth are turning to music as a venue for their creativity with a growing number of performance bands emerging from the Hmong communities in Central California. These bands are hoping for the same type of crossover into the American mainstream that Latin music has enjoyed in recent years.

Chapter 4: Accomplished Hmong Americans

1. Vang Pao: War Veteran and Lobbyist   **141**

Tony Kennedy and Paul McEnroe

The leader of the Hmong that fought the Viet Cong in Laos now lobbies in Washington on behalf of the Hmong in America and Thailand.

2. Mee Moua: Member of State Congress   **154**

Mee Moua

A refugee from Thailand, she emigrated to the United States, and as a politician became the first Hmong member of State Congress.

3. Tou Ger Xiong: Rapper and Comedian   **158**

Nzong Xiong

A professional entertainer who works to bridge the cultural gap through rap music, storytelling, and humor. His message of making peace with your neighbors and respecting humanity has taken him across the country performing and educating people in his cultural traditions.

4. Xa Xiong: Doctor   **161**
   Wendy Harris
   Fleeing from Laos with his family in 1975, he now works
   as a doctor, educating the medical community in Wisconsin on how to care for the Hmong by learning essential communication techniques, and working with the
   traditional shaman.

5. Bill Yang: Entrepreneur   **165**
   Sheryl Jean
   He built a thriving computer business in Wisconsin called
   Hmongmedia Interactive. He now works to link Hmong
   businesses together to help bring prosperity to his people.

Chronology   **169**

For Further Research   **174**

Index   **178**

Foreword

In her popular novels, such as *The Joy Luck Club* and *The Bonesetter's Daughter*, Chinese American author Amy Tan explores the complicated cultural and social differences between Chinese-born mothers and their American-born daughters. For example, the mothers eat foods and hold religious beliefs that their daughters either abhor or abstain from, while the daughters pursue educational and career opportunities that were not available to the previous generation. Generation gaps occur in almost all families, but as Tan's writings show, such differences are even more pronounced when parents grow up in a different country. When immigrants come to the United States, their initial goal is often to start a new life that is an improvement from the life they experienced in their homeland. However, while these newcomers may intend to fully adapt to American culture, they inevitably bring native customs with them. Immigrants have helped make America broader culturally by introducing new religions, languages, foods, and different ways of looking at the world. Their children and subsequent generations, however, often seek to cast aside these traditions and instead more fully absorb mainstream American mores.

As Tan's writings suggest, the dissimilarities between immigrants and their children are manifested in several ways. Adults who come to the United States and do not learn English turn to their children, educated in the American school system, to serve as interpreters and translators. Children, seeing what their American-born schoolmates eat, reject the foods of their native land. Religion is another area where the generation gap is particularly pronounced. For example, the liturgy of Syrian Christian services had to be translated into English when most young Syrian Americans no longer knew how to speak Syriac. Numerous Jews, freed from the European

11

ghettos they had lived in, wished to assimilate more fully into the surrounding culture and began to loosen the traditional dietary and ritual requirements under which they had grown up. Reformed Judaism, which began in Germany, thus found a strong foothold among young Jews born in America.

However, no generational experiences have been as significant as that between immigrant mothers and their daughters. Living in the United States has afforded girls and young women opportunities they likely would not have had in their homelands. The daughters of immigrants, in some cases, live entirely different lives than their mothers did in their native nations. Where an Arab mother may have only received a limited education, her American-raised daughter enjoys a full course of American public schooling, often continuing on to college and careers. A woman raised in India might have been placed in an arranged marriage, while her daughter will have the opportunity to date and choose a husband. Admittedly, not all families have been willing to give their daughters all these new freedoms, but these American-born girls are frequently more willing to declare their wishes.

The generation gap is only one aspect of the immigrant experience in the United States. Understanding immigrants' unique and shared experiences and their contributions to American life is an interesting way to study the many people who make up the American citizenry. Greenhaven Press's Coming to America series helps readers learn why more people have moved to the United States than to any other nation. Selections on the lives of immigrants once they have reached America, from their struggles to find employment to their experiences with discrimination and prejudice, help give students insights into stereotypes and cultural mores that continue to this day. Finally, profiles of prominent immigrants help the reader become aware of the many achievements of these people in fields ranging from science to politics to sports.

Each volume in the Coming to America series takes an extensive look into a particular immigrant population. The carefully selected primary and secondary sources provide both historical perspectives and firsthand insights into the immigrant experience. Combined with an in-depth introduction and a comprehensive chronology and bibliography, every book in the series is a valuable addition to the study of American history. With immigrants comprising nearly 12 percent of the U.S. population, and their children and grandchildren constantly adding to the population, the immigrant experience continues to evolve. Coming to America is consequently a beneficial tool for not only understanding America's past but also its future.

Introduction

In November 2004 a Hmong hunter in Wisconsin named Chai Vang was caught between two worlds; his war-torn homeland and his new home in America. During a hunting expedition, he got lost on private land. His unfortunate interactions with the landowners led to a shooting spree that left six people dead and several others wounded.

His story shocked a nation. Many people inside the Hmong community believed that this type of national publicity would make it more difficult for their brethren already combating stereotypical race bias. According to reporter Jeff Lindsay:

> Importantly, the Hmong community is not making excuses for his action, and strongly condemns the killings. Both Anglos and Hmong grieve over what happened. This incident is a bizarre exception that is in no way characteristic of Hmong people and culture. Hmong hunters and Hmong people in general do not have a track record of striking out in violence against whites. They are not crazies who can be easily provoked into murder.[1]

While this is true, it was difficult for a community of nearly invisible people to stand up to this kind of negative publicity. No polls have been taken of Americans to know the exact figures, but if you do not live within a few miles of a large and thriving Hmong community in America, chances are your knowledge of the Hmong people and their involvement in the Vietnam War is limited at best. Researcher and author James Emery said: "Most Americans don't know who the Hmong are, much less what they sacrificed supporting the United States during the Vietnam War." [2]

The first generation Hmong started their lives in America as invisible, having been thrust from their homeland by a war that the U.S. leaders of the time did not want revealed. Their transition from their traditional culture to American culture has made it a struggle to establish a greater awareness of their story outside their small but growing communities.

The Hmong and the CIA

During the Geneva Conference of 1954 the United States was forbidden by the international community to take an active role in military actions in Laos. The U.S. government and the CIA, however, were worried about the spread of communism in southeast Asia, led by the Soviet Union. The Vietnam War was heating up, and the Ho Chi Minh trail, which served as North Vietnam's main military supply line, passed through Laos. To completely disrupt the supply chain, Americans would have to take the fight into Laos. So in 1965, at the height of the cold war, members of the CIA formed a pact with the Hmong in Laos and Vietnam. CIA representatives told the Hmong that if they would act as a hidden fighting arm of the United States and help with the disruption of the Ho Chi Minh trail, the United States would give the Hmong trainers, munitions, and staples to wage the battles, and protection if the effort failed.

The CIA promises to the Hmong were not kept. Unfortunately, the war in Laos was never meant to be won; the CIA set limits on military actions and targets the Hmong could attack, in order to help hide the U.S. involvement in the Laotian war and keep the battles at a standoff.

In early 1975 the Communist insurgency in Laos, called the Khmer Rouge (Pathet Lao), took possession of Phnom Penh, the capital of Laos. As the new ruling power in Laos, the Khmer Rouge declared the Hmong people enemies of the state and announced they would kill all Hmong found in Laos. In what is now known as the "Killing Fields" an estimated 1.7 million people were killed, including a large and uncounted number of Hmong. At least thirty thousand Hmong were slaughtered immediately. Shortly after this time the United States pulled out of southeast Asia, leaving the Hmong without aid or transport and effectively breaking its promise to take care of the Hmong.

More than one hundred thousand Hmong fled from Laos to Thailand. The Thai government did not want the refugees within their borders. The refugees were kept from integrating into Thailand's cities and instead were forced to stay near the borders, forming ad hoc refugee camps. These camps and the Hmong refugees in them turned into a political hot potato for the United States. The Thai government began the fight to either move the Hmong and other ethnic groups from Laos to other countries or to force their repatriation back to Laos. Because of the resulting international battle many people were stuck living in squalor in Thai refugee camps for over twenty years.

A large unreported number of Hmong who were unable to leave Laos during this time were subsequently killed or imprisoned. In 1978 another large number of Hmong were killed from the use of a chemical weapon known as "Yellow Rain." The exact number killed is unknown. Reporter Anthony Lo-Baido explains that during this time:

> Numerous biochemists, medical doctors and military experts have confirmed the use of Yellow Rain and other toxins against the Hmong. Yet, the U.S. State Department refuses to officially endorse these findings, nor condemn either the Russians or Pathet Lao for using them. In fact, dissenting opinions on the biological warfare claim that the "Yellow Rain" was nothing more than bee pollen and/or bee feces.[3]

In 1980 another wave of a hundred thousand Hmong refugees left Laos for Thailand, putting further pressure on the international community. Resulting investigations in 1981 led scientists for the United Nations to confirm that "Yellow Rain" was used on the Hmong in Laos and the United States could no longer hide behind the "bee pollen" theory.

In 1995 the Thai government officially closed most Laotian refugee camps inside its borders The Hmong that were unable to immigrate to other countries or escape into hiding were forced back to Laos where reports of torture, imprisonment, and death are still coming from the area.

The United States Begins to Right Its Wrongs

Near the end of 1975 the U.S. government became one of a group of countries agreeing to accept Hmong refugees. Out of the more than 100,000 Hmong refugees in the camps at that time, the United States accepted 3,466.

A second wave of immigrants came to the United States in 1978. These refugees were spread throughout the United States in an attempt to mitigate the financial burden on any one state. The Hmong, however, did not like being separated from family members and moved around until most of them were resettled in Minnesota, Wisconsin, or California. Today, these states house more than 80 percent of the Hmong in America.

Mounting political pressure from lobbyists and politicians from these states caused the U.S. Congress to pass the 1980 Refugee Act. Among other things, this act created the Federal Refugee Resettlement Program. It also provided for the effective resettlement of refugees, giving them assistance to achieve self-sufficiency as soon as possible upon arrival. To accomplish this goal, a new office within the Department of Health and Human Services was established called the Office of Refugee Resettlement. This office would fund and administer federal aid programs. The act also formally accepted the definition of "refugee" passed by the United Nations in 1967.

This was a major and welcome change in U.S. policy for the Hmong. It paved the way for more Hmong refugees to enter the United States over the next several years. Though the act did not accomplish as much as many people had hoped, it did provide aid and a structure for the administration of these relief funds. U.S. attorney Harvey Gee said in the year 2000:

> A close reading of the legislative history of the Refugee Act reveals some support for the popular perception held by many that Congress implemented the Act to move the United States into accord with the obligation imposed under international refugee law, which for the first time created a general right to apply for asylum in the United States for non-citizens fleeing political and related prosecutions in their homelands. The reality, however, is that the Refugee Act provided strict controls on the admission of Vietnamese.[4]

Despite its administrative and political difficulties, this act was renewed in 2002 so the government could continue giving aid to the Hmong and other southeast Asian refugees in the United States.

More Hmong refugees trickled into America, and by 1991 there were over one hundred thousand Hmong living in the United States, including second-generation Hmong born within American borders. In 1997, with their numbers growing, continued pressure on the U.S. government caused Washington to officially recognize the Hmong guerrilla veterans of the Laotian war. This opened a path for Congress to pass a bill (H.R. 371) in 2000 that grants these veterans expedited status for U.S. naturalization. The latest round of immigration took place in 2003 when the last remaining Thai refugee camp was closed, and fifteen thousand Hmong came to America.

The Challenge of Assimilation

Many important issues have made assimilation difficult for the Hmong in America. First of all, their language is radically different from English in ways that make English hard to learn. The native Hmong language is monosyllabic, meaning words have only one syllable. It is also a tonal language, where one word can have multiple meanings depending upon how it is spoken. A handbook for teaching English to Hmong-speaking students cites the following example:

> In Hmong, a particular tone is associated with each syllable and the syllable must be pronounced with this tone. For example, in Hmong the word Ma has different meanings depending upon whether a high, mid or low tone is used when saying the word. In Hmong there are eight different tones (compared to 5 in Vietnamese and 6 in Laotian). The 8 different tones include the following—a high tone, a high falling tone, a mid-rising tone, a mid tone, a breathy mid low tone, a low tone, and low falling tone.[5]

Hmong words also do not have inflected forms. There are no plurals, no possessives, no present, past, or future tenses. All meanings are derived by the construction of single-syllable words. This is so radically different from English that it has placed a nearly insurmountable language barrier on many first-generation immigrants.

To make matters worse, the very young first-generation Hmong and the second-generation Hmong are living lives that their parents could barely begin to understand. First-generation Hmong, for the most part, came from a culture without schools, radios, televisions, fast food, electricity, stoves, political democracy, indoor plumbing, computers, libraries, and the influence of other vastly different cultures. First-wave Hmong refugees came without skills to cope with raising children under these circumstances. The children, very early in their lives, tended to reject their parents' traditions in favor of the freer and more modern culture around them.

Of course, each new wave of immigrants came with more and more skills acquired in the refugee camps of Thailand. That, and the fact that each new wave has had the help and support of an ever larger established Hmong community, has over the years made assimilation less of a challenge.

An Industrial Divide

Being a refugee is not new to the Hmong. They have been refugees since at least 2700 B.C. when they were forced from their homes in the upper Yellow River region of China. There is much evidence that they were already refugees at that point, having settled in the upper Yellow River region after being forced from their Siberian homeland a few hundred years before that. This refugee lifestyle established their long-standing nomadic traditions.

Most first-generation Hmong came to America with no industrial skills. Before the Laotian war the Hmong were still living a largely agrarian lifestyle. Even their traditional slash-and-burn farming methods were not acceptable in America. It can be difficult finding work in a modern city if you do not have any experience living in one.

On top of all these obstacles, the Hmong were isolated by their refugee status for such a long time that their spiritual traditions do not resemble those of any other modern culture. Traditions such as animal sacrifice are largely illegal in America, making it difficult to adhere to traditional rituals. The underlying belief that all maladies and difficulties people experience are due to the loss of a person's spirit make it hard for the Hmong to accept modern medicine. Christine Desan describes the Hmong religion as follows:

> This religious system recognizes a duality of body and soul. The Hmong religion blends animism, which provides a practical "body" of rules and regulations, with shamanism, which supplies a theory of the soul. Animism posits an "animated" universe, in which humanity can dwell happily only by dwelling harmoniously. It supplies guidelines for safe behavior among a myriad of spirits and forces. Shamanism complements animism, for while the latter includes basic rules of conduct, standard rituals, and the elementary interpretation of dreams and omens, only the shaman can see, understand, and communicate with the supernatural. It is

the shaman then who guides the dead to rest, who heals the sick (since illness is usually caused by some conflict between the person and the spirits), and who guides the community to auspicious activities.[6]

Many Hmong have since converted to other world religions such as Christianity and Buddhism, but even among these converts, many Hmong still adhere to the shamanistic traditions on the side.

Building Strategies for a Successful Hmong Future in America

There are now more than 175,000 Hmong in America. As these refugees and their children continue to acquire skills and become strong and independent members of society, several strategies have developed to address ongoing challenges.

Many Hmong immigrants continue to suffer psychological stress and trauma related to the mass genocide perpetrated on the Hmong after the end of the Laotian war, as well as the continued reports of internment and death of relatives remaining in Laos. Efforts are being made to provide grief counseling that may help the Hmong to move forward, but these efforts are often hampered by traditional religious beliefs that only shamans can restore the spirit of people affected by this cultural grief.

To counterbalance a lack of education and ensure that the concerns of the Hmong are addressed, a cultural emphasis is placed on higher education for second and subsequent generations of Hmong. These well-educated members of the community are entering every area of American society. For example, many of the educated are entering politics in hope of providing a base of power to their growing communities. Political power coupled with monetary power provided by thriving Hmong businesses are rapidly changing the opportunities open to new Hmong generations.

The Hmong familial structure is also adapting to a more American model. Whereas the first-generation Hmong were accustomed to living in family settlements governed by the male elders of the tribe, most second-generation Hmong are now adopting the same nuclear family structure of the society around them. Hmong are also living, socializing, and intermarrying with other ethnic groups.

Large groups of first-generation, uneducated Hmong women in settlements such as Seattle, Washington, are beginning the movement toward monetary independence. These women have found that their traditional skills of making clothing and other usable artifacts can be lucrative when sold as indigenous folk art.

Educated Hmong women are also finding that they have a power never afforded women in their traditional culture. They are free to decide whom they will marry if they marry at all. They are free to obtain higher education, to enter politics, and to own businesses. This is by far the biggest change in the Hmong social structure and is probably the best hope for the invisible Hmong in America to become free, independent, and visible.

Notes

1. Jeff Lindsay. "Culture Clash: The Hmong in America," Hmong in America, 2006. www.jefflindsay.com/hmong-clash.html. [last updated June 25, 2006]
2. James Emery, "Their World Not Ours—Problems Grip Hmong in America," *World and I*, vol. 17, 2002, p. 170.
3. Anthony LoBaido, "Killing Fields, Mines and Martyrs: Part 2," *World Net Daily*, 1999. www.worldnetdaily.com/news/article.asp?ARTICLE_ID=17254.
4. Harvey Gee, "The Refugee Burden: A Closer Look at the Refugee Act of 1980," *North Carolina Journal of International Law and Commercial Regulation*, vol. 26, 2000, p. 559.
5. Bruce Thowpaou Bliatout, Bruce T. Downing, Judy Lewis, and Dao Yang, *Handbook for Teaching Hmong-Speaking Students*, 1988, Folsom Cordova Unified School District, 1988, pp. 48–59.
6. Christine Desan, "A Change of Faith for Hmong Refugees," *Cultural Survival*, vol. 7, no. 3, pp. 45–48, 1983.

COMING *TO* AMERICA

CHAPTER 1

At War in Laos

The Secret U.S. Pact with the Hmong in Laos

Amoun Vang Sayaovong

In 1996 a landmark speech was delivered to a group of Hmong Americans by former Central Intelligence Agency (CIA) chief William E. Colby, describing a secret pact between the United States and the Hmong in Laos. As Colby recounted, in 1962 President John F. Kennedy asked the CIA to find people in Laos willing to fight against Communists infiltrating in Laos from Vietnam. The CIA secretly recruited the Hmong to fight with military aid from the United States, thus creating a clandestine army hidden from world view. To adhere to the spirit of the Geneva Accords of 1962, the agreement that ended the war between France and Laos, the Hmong were only allowed to fight defensively and could not launch any offensives against North Vietnam. With these restrictions, the Hmong successfully held back North Vietnamese aggressors but suffered severe casualties. When the war in Vietnam ended in 1975, and American forces pulled out of Southeast Asia, the Hmong were left with little alternative but to flee their country.

In this selection Amoun Vang Sayaovong discusses Colby's speech and provides further information about the role of the Hmong in fighting the North Vietnamese encroachment into Laos. He describes the extensive cover-up to keep the American people from learning of the U.S. involvement in the war efforts. William Sullivan, deputy assistant secretary of state for East Asia even testifies to the U.S. Senate Foreign Relations Subcommittee that there was no pact between the United States and the Hmong at all.

Amoun Vang Sayaovong, "William Colby, the Hmong and the CIA," *Ink*, vol. 1, spring 1997. Copyright 1997 INK: Hmong Magazine. Reproduced by permission.

Sayaovong, a first-generation Hmong immigrant in America, is a board member and secretary of the United Hmong Coalition, a group dedicated to increasing Hmong participation in politics.

In 1962, with few viable options, President John F. Kennedy asked the Central Intelligence Agency (CIA) to find people in Laos who valued their independence enough to resist the North Vietnamese encroachment into their country.

With that order, two agents contacted the Hmong, recounted former CIA chief William E. Colby to a small group of mainly Hmong students who had gathered at the Georgetown Hmong Youth Conference.

The events Colby spoke of transpired some thirty years ago during the time of their parents, long before any of these students had been born. So appropriately enough, it was in this room at Georgetown University last April [1996]—surrounded by the very children of transplanted Hmong veterans the CIA recruited to fight the "secret war" in Laos—that Colby's long, distinguished life came full circle.

No one knew it at the time but unfortunately, this would be Colby's last public speaking engagement. Just three weeks after filling in important gaps in the formation of the CIA's relationship with these students' parents, Colby was found dead in the Potomac River, the victim of a ruptured aneurysm.

As one of the less than twenty people present at his last speech, it was a true pleasure to meet the man and to have him place the Laotian war into the larger context of the worldwide conflict in Southeast Asia. The following analysis presents parts of Colby's speech along with other evidence that will help clarify the conflict in Laos and the Hmong role.

The Trauma of War

As with the Hmong, the Vietnam War remains a traumatic period in history for many Americans. The aftershocks of the

American effort to contain communism in Southeast Asia continue to be felt to this day. In just two decades, a whole new community with an ancient culture was transplanted from one world to another. Twenty years ago, many Americans would not have known who a "Hmong" person was.

Today, the Hmong inhabit all regions of the United States—and all five continents. For the Hmong people, the drama in Laos remains at the center of attention. Fighting the secret war in Laos forced the Hmong to assume many roles and identities; from highland farmers they became guerrilla warfare specialists, then refugees fleeing genocide and finally the Hmong found themselves taking on the role of immigrants, adopting new homes around the world. It is this understanding of Hmong history that one must have to truly know the significance of the Hmong people in Colby's speech.

Colby is better known for giving away the CIA's "family jewels," top-level cloak-and-dagger secrets which included plots to topple foreign governments and schemes of assassination. His importance to Hmong history however, lies in his revelations about the American government's policy position with respect to Laos. What was America doing in Laos, a small country of only three million people, full of mountains and as backward as any third world country?

After two decades, the Hmong are still uncertain as to why the Americans turned to them for help against the Communists. The origin of the relationship between the Hmong and the United States can be traced to events that began before 1962 which culminated in the signing of the Geneva Accords.

The Geneva Accords

Before 1962, American, Soviet, Chinese and North Vietnamese military and paramilitary forces were all present in Laos. American policy-makers became concerned with the possibility of military confrontation between the superpowers. To them, the consequences of such an encounter could have disastrous results, as three of the four countries possessed nuclear capabilities.

"President Kennedy and General Secretary Khrushchev [of] the Soviet Union had a meeting in 1961," Colby explained. "They both agreed, we were going to have our confrontations. Laos [was] not the place for it. Let's recognize a neutral and independent Laos, withdraw all our military and para-military forces, just leave it alone and leave it out of the equation."

General agreements from that meeting resulted in the signing of the Geneva Accords in 1962. In itself, the primary goal of the Accords was simple and symbolic: it expressed the mutual American and Soviet interest in avoiding possible confrontation in the tiny country by broadly prohibiting all nations from interfering in the affairs of Laos. Specifically, it required all nations to remove non-diplomatic personnel from Laotian soil.

Ensuring Compliance

To ensure compliance, Canada, India and Poland were selected to the ICC or International Commission for Supervision and Control of Laos. Its duty: to monitor and report violations of the Accords to the signatory countries.

In theory, the carefully chosen members of the ICC—one communist state (Poland), one American-allied state (Canada) and one supposedly neutral state (India)—was to secure fair and equal representation from the two principle governing/social theories, democracy and communism. One system was not to gain an advantage over the other. In practice however, the United States felt that India leaned favorably toward communism. This bias on India's behalf quickly presented the Americans with a major obstacle.

Pursuant to the agreement, the USSR, China and the United States all withdrew their troops. But when the North Vietnamese dishonored the Accords and removed only forty soldiers from a force of 7,000, American policy-makers faced the first of a series of major dilemmas. As feared, despite obvious breech of international agreement by North Vietnam, the ICC stalled investigations and failed to rigorously enforce treaty conditions. At the same time, the United States could not reintroduce American troops into Laos to force compliance with the Geneva Accords without breaking the treaty themselves. Such a move risked drawing Chinese and Soviet military presence back into Laos.

An Alliance Is Born

Keeping with policy, the American government didn't want to risk unnecessary military confrontation with the other two world powers. However, the United States still needed to prevent the North Vietnamese from helping the communist Pathet Lao take over Laos. It was within this global context that forged the alliance between the United States and the Hmong. The 1962 Geneva Accords proscribed the manner in which the Americans could help the Hmong and the type of war the Hmong would be required to fight.

"We began to get the signals in 1962 after the agreement [Geneva Accords] that the North Vietnamese were beginning to move. They were beginning to build up their forces. They were beginning to move out of the area Nam Sam Neau and so forth, down towards the Plain de Jars. They began to push the Hmong around. . . . He [President Kennedy] said: 'CIA, can you provide a little quiet help to the people in Laos who want to fight for their own independence?' and our two officers were in contact with the Hmong," Colby recounted.

"They said, 'Yes, the Hmong want to fight.' They wanted to defend their territory against these North Vietnamese who were beginning to push down into them and that was basically the origin of the [Hmong/CIA] relationship."

Concealment

American desire to adhere to the spirit of the Geneva Accords deemed it necessary that the Hmong serve as a clandestine force which could harass the North Vietnamese without being directly linked to the United States. The Hmong were prohibited from taking any offensive actions as that could lead to an escalation in the war on the part of the North Vietnamese. Increased fighting also had the potential to expose the American support of the Hmong and could possibly lead to a complete annulment of the Geneva Accords. Colby—then CIA Deputy Director—was instructed by Assistant Secretary W. Averell Harriman of the State Department to keep the effort in Laos purely defensive in nature.

"'Okay, one hundred guns but no attacks, only for defense,'" Colby said of Harriman's orders. "Don't get the Hmong to do any attack against the North Vietnamese. We don't want to escalate this thing any more than possible," explained Colby of the American policy in the 1960s. "We would just like to dampen it down where it is . . . where we don't let it get any further but we don't try to win any victories there [Laos]."

The need to conceal American involvement in Laos was also substantiated by the testimony of William Sullivan, Deputy Assistant Secretary of State for East Asian and Pacific Affairs.

Denial of Commitment to War

In October of 1969, Sullivan was questioned by the Counsel Roland A. Paul before a Senate Foreign Relations subcommittee on the United States's commitment to the Hmong.

Paul asked of Sullivan: "So the presence of American military forces in Laos is not in itself a commitment-generating factor?" "We do not consider that it is a commitment," Sullivan replied. Paul clarified his own question: "Would this mean that we could increase our military presence in stages in Laos with the ability to terminate that augmentation at any time?" "I believe that we have that ability currently. In fact, we used to use [as] a rule of thumb our ability to make it reversible and terminate it within eight hours," Sullivan answered. "It would probably take 24 hours now, but it still could be done."

From the very beginning the United States was interested in maintaining the neutrality of Laos. American diplomats negotiated the Geneva Accords in good faith not knowing beforehand that the North Vietnamese would not honor the agreement. Even in supporting Hmong, the United States tried to hold to the spirit of the Accords by discouraging the Hmong from taking the offensive. American forces in Laos were held to a 24-hour rule, partly to minimize the chances of detection.

Denial of Commitment to the Hmong

What was the commitment of the United States with respect to the Hmong given the American desire for neutrality?

[As] Sullivan testified in 1969, there was no commitment to the Hmong from day to day. The relationship between the Hmong and the United States served the greater purpose of keeping Laos neutral. The Americans assumed the attitude that the Hmong had lived on this land long enough to defend it against foreign encroachment. According to Colby, from an American policy-making standpoint, the arrangement appeared mutually beneficial.

The United States provided the munitions and general directions but left the decisions up to the Hmong. It was an arrangement that suited the Hmong perfectly. Being intensely independent, fighting the war as they saw fit was a level of control that few Hmong leaders had ever experienced before. With American aid, the Hmong advanced rapidly beyond the limits imposed on them by Laotian society. At this basic level of analysis, the relationship served both sides well.

However, given that the secret war in Laos was dictated to be a stalemate by the American interest in preserving the neutrality of Laos, what would have been the fate of the Hmong in Laos if the war had not ended? Since the Hmong were expected to fight a purely defensive war, there was no chance the North Vietnamese would ever be driven out of Laos. The war in Laos could have continued without a final resolution. But by the close of the war in Laos, the age[s] of some of the front-line Hmong troops were starting to dip into the low teens. The estimated casualties sustained by Hmong forces by 1969 was 18,000. From such sobering facts, it is evident that the Hmong could not have sustained a defensive war indefinitely, regardless of US or Hmong desire to continue such a fight.

Struggle to Understand

Colby maintains that the defensive strategy devised by the CIA and employed by the United States was ultimately in the best interest of the Hmong. "I have to say that that was good for Laos, and for the Hmong. You were not subjected to the massive kind of military contest that might have developed otherwise, including the massive destruction that [a major war effort] brings," Colby said.

It will never be known how a full-scale war would have affected the Hmong in Laos. Were more Hmong lives saved because the situation never escalated beyond a minor war in a backward, agrarian country? What did happen was that support from the United States ended with the commencement of the Paris peace talks with the North Vietnamese, Laos fell to communism and the Hmong had no alternatives but to flee in masses.

More than two decades after the war in Laos, the Hmong continue to struggle to understand the war and their role in it. Many in the Hmong community still claim the war could have been won. However, given the limitations placed upon

American support, there is little doubt that if the war could have been won by Hmong forces alone, it would have been won at a tremendous cost in Hmong lives. It is about time that the Hmong community know the complete truth about the war in Laos. Knowing the truth will finally allow the older generation to put to rest any feelings that they lost a war. Knowing the truth will give the new generations respect for their people and their origin.

Colby's final remarks reflect many of the American voices who worked with, fought alongside, and died with the tens of thousands of Hmong in Laos: "As an American, I for one am delighted that our country has been strengthened by the addition of people like yourselves. You can be good Hmong and at the same time, you can be good Americans. You can be both," Colby said. "And I think you will be."

The Hmong Flee Laos

Gary Yia Lee

The war in Vietnam was declared over in 1975. Fearing retribution from the Pathet Lao—the new governing regime in Laos—many Hmong flooded into Thailand. Despite the fact that Thailand did not want these refugees, it did not take long for large encampments to form. Thailand tried to stop the influx of Hmong by putting up barriers such as announcing that if Laotian refugees came across their border, they would not be given access to resettlement camps. The Hmong who stayed in Laos suffered abuse, incarceration, and death.

In this selection Gary Yia Lee describes the circumstances of the end of the war and the severe retributions of the Pathet Lao. He estimates that over fifty thousand Hmong died at the hands of the Pathet Lao before they had an opportunity to flee. He also discusses the movement of refugees from Laos to Thailand and how they settled in camps. He also includes an accounting of the number of refugees sent to other countries, including the United States.

Lee is a scholar with degrees in social work and anthropology. He is also a founding member of the Hmong-Australian Society, a group that helps Hmong immigrants in Australia succeed in their new home. He has also been involved in settlement work among Lao and other Indonesian refugees since 1976.

Fearing retributions from the new regime after the PL [Pathet Lao] control of Laos, many former RLA [Republic of Laos] Hmong soldiers and civilians who could not flee to Thailand went into hiding with their families in inaccessible mountain areas. They were joined by others who were released or who escaped from "seminar" centres. From their jungle hide-outs, small groups of these men first ambushed PL trucks travelling between Vang Vieng and Vientiane in early 1976, but soon included PL troops in their attacks. They repeatedly used arms and ammunitions left hidden by [Hmong leader] Vang Pao in Phu Bia or collected from their dead victims.

Although American diplomats in Laos disclaimed any involvement with these tribal dissidents, reports about their skirmishes filtered through to the outside world throughout 1976. Armed resistance was also reported in Sayaboury [in Laos] where refugees in Thailand were said to return to Laos and carry out their separate campaign against PL and Vietnamese soldiers. Initial casualties on the government side were believed to include two Soviet helicopters and crew, in addition to "serious losses" suffered by village militia and local military personnel.

Pathet Lao Sends in Troops

The Government decided to send troops to the hills to crush this resistance. When they proved ineffective, four regiments of NV [North Vitnamese] soldiers were brought in from other parts of Laos. Many Hmong settlements were burned to the ground, sometimes accompanied by mass execution of their inhabitants. Aerial bombing was carried out along with heavy artillery lifted to the highlands by helicopters. Poisonous chemicals were alleged to have been dropped on civilians hiding in the jungles and defoliants were sprayed on their crops. Those who surrendered themselves to the authorities were taken to "resettlement villages" in the lowlands where they were selected for "seminars", imprisonment or executions, depending on the decisions of the military.

This pattern of resistance and government counter-attacks persists even today, and is one the major causes of the continuing refugee movement to Thailand. The resistance has been further fuelled by political groups formed by Lao refugees who have resettled in the West, among which was the United Front for the Liberation of Laos under Vang Pao's leadership. Border Thai intelligence officers have also played an ongoing role in this resistance by supplying small groups of refugees with arms and sending them back to Laos to gather military information, thereby putting into jeopardy the lives of villagers who come into contact with these teams. The only recourse for such villagers is to escape to Thailand with their families in order to avoid persecution by PL officials.

Official estimates put the number of Hmong dissidents killed in the military operations of 1977 at 1,300 and "thousands" captured in "heavy fighting" [according to the December 16, 1979, issue of *Asia Week*]. On his part, Vang Pao alleged that 50,000 Hmong died from PL chemical poisoning between 1975 and 1978, while another 45,000 perished "from starvation and diseases or were shot trying to escape to Thailand". Whatever the number of casualties, there is no doubt that the campaign against Hmong and other dissidents had significantly increased the number of people crossing to Thailand. One group of 2,500 Hmong, for instance, arrived in Nong Khai refugee camp in December 1977. This was the biggest single escape party which was said to number more than 8,000 members when it first set out from Phu Bia, but a number of them changed their mind and returned to their jungle hide-outs while many others were captured, died from exhaustion, shot by PL troops along the escape route, or drowned trying to swim across the Mekong River.

Refugees Resettle around the World

Since 1980, some of these refugees have included people who had traditionally aligned with the PL and many families which had been living in the 'new liberated zone'. From the first group of 25,000 Hmong reaching Thailand in May 1975, the number had steadily increased to 60,000 towards the end of 1979 when close to 3,000 persons crossed the Mekong a month. It is estimated that by 1990, more than 90,000 Hmong refugees have gone to live in the United States; 6,000 in France; and 3,000 in Canada, Australia, Argentina and French Guyana. Another 60,000 lowland Lao have also been resettled in the West, mostly in the United States (35,000); France (16,000); Canada (4,000), and Australia (8,600). About 3,000 had voluntarily been repatriated to Laos under UNHCR [United Nations High Commission for Refugees] auspice, but some are known to have escaped to Thailand again.

The total number of Hmong refugees in Thai camps in March 1980 was 48,937 persons with 998 new arrivals during that month. Despite departures for resettlement in other countries, there were still 46,218 Hmong registered for support by the United Nations High Commission for Refugees in five camps in Northern Thailand in February 1981. About 75,000 Lao refugees were known to be in Thailand in 1987, the largest group of Indochinese refugees under UNHCR protection. Of this number, 54,095 were hill tribe people, mostly Hmong being held at Ban Vinai and Chiang Kham camps. At the end of 1990, there were still 22,000 lowland Lao refugees in Ban Napho camp; 40,000 Hmong at Ban Vinai (including 10,000 unregistered new arrivals); 22,000 in Chiang Khan and another 5,000 awaiting to go to third countries in Phanat Nikhom camp.

The reasons for refugees continuing to leave Laos have remained much the same since 1975: persecution against former RLG officials, military offensives directed at resistance groups, heavy rice tax, military and labour conscription, extreme economic deprivation, and arbitrary arrests of people suspected of political crimes or disloyalty. Many of the right-wing politicians, army officers and public servants taken to "seminar" centres have been released, with some subsequently escaping to join their families in Thailand and the West. Other internees, including the former King and Queen and the Crown

Prince, are known to have died from hard labour and the harsh conditions of the re-education camps, and about 200 still remain in detention.

The Pathet Lao Tighten Restrictions

The Pathet Lao have taken control of Laos since 1975, but refugees continue to flow to Thailand, especially the hill tribes. This is despite many deterrents put in place by the Thai government such as keeping refugees in closed camps with no access to resettlement in other countries in order to prevent further flows from Laos; the tightening of the definition of the term "refugee" and classifying most Lao as "economic" rather than political refugees; and forcing people back to Laos after they have crossed into Thailand. Since 1987, there has been a relaxation in the Lao government's policy with family businesses and commercial enterprises being allowed to flourish, more freedom of movements in and out of the country, and more tourism and trade with Thailand. This new policy, however, has been affected by the recent political change in Eastern Europe and the Soviet Union which used to be the major aid donors and ideological supporters of the Pathet Lao. During the second half of 1990, the government decided to return to a stricter rule with many arrests of senior officials suspected of "liberal" thinking, and a tighter control of population movements due to increased insurgency activities by resistance groups across the country. So long as the country's leaders do not learn to accommodate to each other but only see armed intervention and arbitrary arrests as the solutions to their differences, Lao refugees will continue to be generated and require international assistance.

The Great Betrayal of the Hmong

Anthony C. LoBaido

When the Hmong were recruited to help fight in Laos, they were promised that the United States would not abandon them. They were promised a home in America with the same benefits given the U.S. military fighters. In the following selection Anthony C. LoBaido describes how the United States did not follow through on those promises at the end of the Vietnam conflict. He also explains how American policies prolonged the end of the war, leaving the Hmong people without many options to assure their survival. LoBaido believes the actions of the United States are shameful and have produced a great and ugly betrayal of a tribal people who were willing to fight and remain loyal to the United States during a time of upheaval.

LoBaido is an investigative reporter for WorldNetDaily, an online resource for world news.

Nakhon Phanom, Thailand—An old Hmong woman sobbed hysterically, burying her face in the hands of her young granddaughter. The United Nations High Commission on Refugees had made its final decision: The woman and her entire extended family would be forcibly repatriated to Communist-ruled Laos—at gunpoint if necessary—by the men in the blue berets.

"No, oh my God, no!" the woman sobbed over and over again. "They're going to kill us all!"

That was the scene at the Ban Napho camp Sept. 29 [1999], where U.N. staff had just finished conducting the last of its "interviews" to determine which Hmong (pronounced "mung") families would be forced to return to Laos.... Few knowledgeable observers are shocked at the Hmong's reluctance to return to their native land.

The Hmong Are Hated in Laos

The Hmong are hated by the power brokers in the Stalinist government that rules Laos today. This hatred is rooted in the Hmong's legendary role in aiding the French colonialists during the Indochina War of the 1950s, and, a decade later, in their having fought alongside the American forces during the Vietnam war. The Hmong were portrayed, although somewhat crudely, in the 1979 Francis Ford Coppola film, "Apocalypse Now."

Today, the Hmong are a besieged people on many fronts. Both medical and military experts claim that the ruling government of Laos has used Russian-made biochemical weapons against the Hmong. UNICEF, the United Nations Children's Fund, currently is engaging in population control efforts against the tribe, trying to limit members to three children per family. And worst of all, the Hmong have found themselves abandoned by the U.S. State Department, CIA and Pentagon—their former patrons. Far from being given a homeland and preferential treatment, as promised, for their past allegiance and military service to America, they are being forced to return to a nation that considers them less than human—to a fate of almost certain extermination.

How Did This Happen?

An amazing and tortured story, it all began when U.S. Army Special Forces soldier Carl Bernard, an experienced infantry captain, was posted to Laos in 1961 with the "White Star Mobile Training Team" from the Army's Special Forces at Fort Bragg.

"The Hmong are rugged mountain people who were trained by the CIA in Special Forces units during the 1960s and 1970s," recalled Bernard. He was the point man on the CIA-U.S. Army's official mission to recruit and train the Hmong to fight against the Communist Viet Cong. Just why was the Army recruiting native hill tribesmen to fight?

Bernard Understands the Hmong Are Needed

Having served in China with the Marines in 1945–46, Bernard was extremely knowledgeable on the long-running regional conflict due to his extensive contacts with French officers involved in the French-Indochina War.

In particular, Bernard was impressed with the explanation of the way Communist China's forces were able to contain, conquer and then convert those of anti-Maoist Chiang Kai-shek into the formidable units that caused the U.S. such staggering losses in the Korean War.

Bernard understood that the United States would need the support of the ethnic hill tribes of Indochina to win the Vietnam war. While the conflict was conventional in nature, there were also unconventional aspects to the war that would definitely swing the balance of the final outcome.

"Army officials had expressed concern to then-President John F. Kennedy about Laos, an unknown country, becoming the first domino in the line," said Bernard in an interview with WorldNetDaily. Therefore, Bernard's own 12-man team was assigned in the northern section of the country with half of them posted to the Hmong, overlooking the Plain of Jars, and the other half assisting in the training of the Lao Royal Army in Luang Prabang.

The French advisers still present were focused only on providing operational advice and assistance. By this time, the French Foreign Legion had been defeated in Indochina by the forerunners of the Viet Cong, and had retreated to fight other battles in North Africa on behalf of the evaporating French empire. If the former French colonies of Laos, Vietnam and

Cambodia were to remain aligned with the West, it was up to Bernard, his fledgling mountain fighters and the American war machine.

"I had the chance to travel extensively with Vang Pao, who had always served as the chief of the Hmong forces. Also traveling with us were senior members of the Royal Army," Bernard recalled.

Bernard Sends Detailed Reports to America

Detailed reports from his visits—on many of which he was the sole "round eye" present—provided a perspective often criticized as making America's policies look doomed to failure.

The U.S. Embassy transformed numerous unfavorable reports about the war into something that evolved into Saigon's "Five O'clock Follies"—fractured and flawed news reports on the war situation. Yet, the content of these reports—with no sources contradicting their message—was adequate to mislead Washington's decision makers into believing that a successful and very inexpensive war effort was being waged, using ignorant and innocent mountain people.

The death of each Hmong Special Forces soldier in the "secret war" in Laos meant one less body bag coming back to the U.S. This was important to Washington, since each American body bag carried with it a political price tag, as the American public grew weary of the war effort.

The Military Industrial Complex Is Making Money

But the war was to drag on for years. "The military industrial complex didn't want to bring the Vietnam war to a swift end," said one Western military attache based in Laos' capital of Vientiane.

"Bell Helicopter and Dow Chemical were making millions in aircraft and Agent Orange [a toxic herbicide]. The elites running the war didn't want to accept that a bunch of half-assed mountain boys like the Hmong could actually turn the tide of the war," he said. "But they took out at least half of all Soviet and Red Chinese supplies headed for the Viet Cong along the Ho Chi Min trail."

So, while the policy makers in the White House and Pentagon debated the merits and viability of the Hmong Special Forces operation, the Hmong fought on with a scarcely believable tenacity.

Yet, they paid a huge price for their allegiance to the American forces. The Hmong were destined to lose one quarter of their entire population, and knew no more of evolving U.S. policies (their eventual betrayal) and practices (fighting to "lose the war" and negotiate a "peace" and eventual withdrawal) than did their mentors from the U.S. Special Forces.

Bernard Is Promoted

Meanwhile, Bernard was promoted to major and returned to Fort Bragg with his team after just six months in Laos. Gen. William P. Yarborough, commander of the Special Forces Warfare Center, agreed that more than perfunctory language and area training were required to help the Hmong hill tribes. Yarborough authorized Bernard to visit anthropology and sociology departments at Duke and the University of North Carolina to determine what could be done to teach soldiers to cross cultures.

"Sadly, the interest of the 'real Army' in such exotic ways to become more effective in the field remained very low. Its real focus was on stopping the Warsaw Pact [the Soviet Union and its allies] from invading Western Europe, not fighting land wars in Asia," lamented Bernard.

As Bernard's time in Vietnam neared its end, he penned a final report on the bipolar strategies of the Pentagon and Viet Cong. In it, he wrote, "The U.S. continues to concentrate the bulk of resources and military might on controlling the terrain and looking for massed enemy formations. The Viet Cong continues to concentrate its talents on controlling the people. Each succeeds."

The Hmong Are Betrayed

Despite the success of the Hmong in attacking the Viet Cong's supply lines in southern Laos, or the horrendous losses they had suffered in the process, Bernard did not realize how deep their betrayal by the U.S. State Department would go.

"The Hmong were expecting that their combat support of the Laos government's American allies would earn them treatment as full citizens. They did not fail as Special Forces soldiers in the field. Their only 'failure' was believing in the Americans' ability to win the war and keep their word," says Bernard.

"The CIA agents who had given them guarantees of their place in the long-term plans of the United States did not have the authority to do this, nor the means to carry out what they promised. These men knew so little of the conflicting Laos and Hmong cultures that their promises were both confused and impossible to fulfill. Yet the Hmong thought of themselves as an American army and believed they would be taken care of."

"Their betrayal is a horrible shame to the United States. It sets a bad example for any potential allies America might well need to fight on our side in a future war. The Kurds come to mind," said Bernard.

The Camps of Thailand

Today, the plight of the Hmong is rapidly intensifying. Since the mid-'70s, the Hmong have lived in refugee camps on the Thai-Laos border. But since 1980, over 24,000 Laotians have been sent back to Laos from Thai refugee camps. Some 324,172 have been repatriated to Western nations like Australia, New Zealand, France and the United States—nations that have sent forces to fight in Indochina since World War II.

But the most current issue pressing the Hmong people involves those still languishing at the Ban Napho camp. The U.N. High Commission on Refugees has stated it will cut off all funding for the Hmong by Dec. 31, 1999. Two more "final redeployments" are expected by that time—that is, the U.N. will send the rest of the camp's Hmong back to Laos in two final groups before year end.

For its part, the Laotian Communist government says it will accept only voluntary returnees, but the refugees say their lives are in danger if they return.

"The Pathet Lao fear a right-wing, Christian, anti-Communist movement by the Hmong," explained Baylor University's award-winning filmmaker, Dr. Michael Korpi. "The Pathet Lao word for the Hmong, 'Meo,' means 'less than human'—and the government will kill them with impunity as it has in the past." Korpi's [1981] documentary film, "City of Refuge," about the repatriated Hmong . . . living in Iowa, has received international acclaim.

Life Is Unsettled in the Camps

Thus, it was no surprise that Thailand's government deployed over 1,000 antiriot police to help quell the hour-long riot that broke out within the Ban Napho camp on the morning of Sept. 29 [1999].

Western journalists were not permitted to enter the camp and speak with the Hmong, but WorldNetDaily did manage to enter undercover and interview a number of the Hmong people there.

"More than 20 of our soldiers have escaped this camp," one Hmong man told WorldNetDaily. "They have been identified as anti-Communists and face certain death upon their return to our homeland."

Those who returned to Laos were given "care packages" of personal health care items and a relocation allowance of one hundred U.S. dollars. According to Lao Communist government officials, the returnees were scheduled to live for the time being at a temporary facility near the village of Ban Na Saat in Khammouane province.

Hmong Do Not Trust Laotion Government

But few Hmong are willing to take the Communist Pathet Lao regime at its word. For example, the Oct. 8 [1999] edition of the Communist Party-controlled *Vientiane Times* said, "The (Sept. 29) repatriation movement took place peacefully and smoothly."

In reality, the exact opposite was the case. The repatriation, carried out by the U.N., Thai government and Pathet Lao Communists, caused a full-scale riot. It was, in fact, only the first in a series of deceptions that likely will lead to the death of many of the other 1,064 Hmong being held in the Ban Napho camp.

"In this age of global media, who wonders at how this final liquidation can be taking place? It is a symbol of the agenda of the United Nations, Clinton administration and U.S. State Department—hatred of Christians and anti-Communists," charged Korpi.

In the end, many Americans might be left wondering how a pantheon of U.S. administrations all could have failed so completely one of America's most courageous and loyal allies.

Disgraceful Behavior

Bernard cites the "shameful avoidance of any responsibility for the betrayal of the Hmong by the Nixon administration, itself focused on getting on with the Chinese. Hence they were unwilling to be diverted for the obligations of this powerless element. Soon after, Jimmy Carter's ability to understand our use of the Hmong was thwarted by the elements of the CIA avoiding responsibility for their situation and keeping the situation covered up as well as they could."

Bernard adds, "The disgraceful repatriation of the Hmong to Laos has shamed our nation since its beginning. It is not a secret, only proof of the power of inertia."

Although the U.S. did repatriate thousands of Hmong back to mid-western U.S. states when the war turned bad, there simply wasn't enough room in the lifeboat. Of those who were brought to the U.S., Bernard said, "the older Hmong in the U.S.A. still hope to return to their beloved hills in the north. Their younger elements are making Americans of themselves."

Today, scores of eligible Hmong living in the U.S. are not receiving the same military benefits as our own combat veterans, even though many of them fought as U.S. combat infantrymen for 10-plus years. Many Americans who fought in the Vietnam war as combat infantrymen were there for only six months.

"I believe that the Hmong will never quit fighting the Pathet Lao—not now, not ever," said Korpi.

Nina Morrison, a former CIA pilot for Air America in Laos during the Vietnam war adds, "I love the Hmong people. And in the hills of Laos, among the clouds, there are many great stories of bravery and betrayal."

For the Hmong people, it would appear that their half-century-old nightmare of warfare and betrayal is only beginning.

CHAPTER 2

COMING TO AMERICA

The Hmong Arrive in America

Hmong Refugees Have Difficulty Assimilating

Suzanne C. Dirks

In Laos the Hmong were an agrarian people living in a prein-dustrialized society with no written language and very few work skills other than farming. In this selection Suzanne C. Dirks ex-plores the difficult transition of the first wave of Hmong immi-grants as they try to assimilate into the highly industrialized world of America. Many reasons this assimilation has been so difficult are explained, including differences in cultural beliefs and lack of education and employable skills. She also presents several suggestions to help ease the difficulties of the Hmong in their quest to become integrated into their new homeland. She suggests that government agencies encourage postsecondary edu-cation, help refugees apply for naturalization, and foster a view-point of the Hmong as a valuable segment of our society.

Dirks wrote the paper from which the following selection is extracted as part of her studies as a graduate student at the Uni-versity of Wisconsin–Stout in the Department of Guidance and Counseling.

Moving from a pre-industrial, pre-literate third world so-ciety to a superpower nation based on machines and education was a rapid adjustment that the Hmong have had to make in just a matter of years. In the transition, the chil-dren have often taken on roles of interpreter and become the sources of information supplied to the families. Many of the elders and parents could not speak English and had difficulty learning the language, and/or had no income. In this patrilinial society, the head of the household was to supply the income and information necessary for the family; not being able to do so caused loss of respect.

Suzanne C. Dirks, "Chapter 2: Review of Literature," *The Hmong: A Human Resource in Transition*, May 1999, p. x-xvi. Reproduced by permission.

The Hmong were a mountain, agrarian people who have for hundreds of years used the slash and burn method of farming. They were subsistence farmers who raised animals for food and/or sometimes trading. Money did not play a major role in their economy. Wealth was expressed with silver coins and jewelry (made of silver and silver coins). The coins were also sewn onto the clothing, but were worn only on special occasions, like the New Year celebrations. They had developed a patrilineal clan system that was the main source of organization within their political, social, economic, and religious systems. Each clan member shared the same patrilineal ancestors. There are 18 clan names with alliances through marriages to assure counsel and support within the great family of Hmong. All persons with the same last name were considered brothers and sisters.

A Hmong household contained a very extended family, with the head of the household retaining final authority. The household served to train the children and placed a very high value on the elders. For the Hmong female, marriage took her from her father's home, and she became the property of the husband's family. The female did not take the husband's name, but all children acquired the father's family name. Polygamy was practiced within the clan system, but was usually a result of a widow's marriage to her late husband's brother. Wealthier men had a number of wives to maintain the kinship system. The group was always considered before the individual. The Hmong religion was the practice of animism, which is ancestral worship. The main theme of animism was to maintain a balance between oneself and the supernatural world. Many Hmong have converted to Christian religious practices and about half of those who emigrated to the US belonged to the Missionary Alliance Denomination.

The Hmong Value Education

In Laos, the established education opportunities for the Hmong were very limited. Children learned skills and oral history from village elders. The Hmong did not have a written language until the late 1950's. When living in Laos, the expense of education allowed few Hmong boys, and rarely girls, to receive formal education. The value of education increased because of that scarcity. Education was the key that opened doors for the Hmong to start breaking the cycle of poverty and public assistance in which they have become entangled in the US. The children were encouraged to excel academically, yet were also expected to help maintain the home. Girls especially were limited in their extra curricular activities and often needed to assist in child care and household chores. The Policy Research Institute Report of April 1991, stated that the standard scores of scholastic performance of the Hmong children were almost 40% higher than the average for all schools. When compared to other Asian Americans, the Hmong were not successful, but they came to this country with less preparation than just about any other group in our history.

Challenges to Hmong Culture

Hmong families who have become involved in mainstream America lose and/or accommodate their traditional values, ceremonies, religion and ethnic heritage. In the US, many elders feel useless in this society as the American values change the lifestyle of the younger Hmong. The goal of the American officials was to resettle the Hmong refugees, and to disperse the population into various locations to avoid overloading any one area. The officials did not understand the clan system. They arranged for private sponsorship and job placement, but again underestimated the language problem and the Hmong necessity to live closer to family.

In 1975, the first Hmong arrived in Wausau [Wisconsin], and according to the Wausau Hmong Association, there were 4,368 Hmong as of March 1998. About 255 Southeast Asian families in Marathon County rely on public assistance. Among the population of the Wausau area, 10% are Southeast Asian, and 90% of that number are Hmong. The older Hmong continue to have difficulty finding employment because of the inability to understand English.

According to [scholar S.K.] Hunter, US children are taught to be aggressive, independent, and self-reliant. For the Hmong children, responsibility to the family comes before the individual. The effect of the American culture is causing tremendous change in behavior in the Hmong homes and can cause disturbances within the family and clans.

Preparing for College

According to [scholar P.] Vang, parents with little educational background are not able to help their children prepare for college. They cannot assist their children in identifying clear goals to work toward higher achievement in college. Traditionally, the head of the household is the final authority, so newly independent students can flounder when they embark on the road to higher education. Decisions are thrust on them and choices need to be made, but often without direction from home. Parents do not understand how the government or educational systems function, and rely on the students to guide them. The students are faced with the financial needs for attaining a post-secondary institution education. The family is very limited in its ability to aid with these needs because of low household income.

The WI [Wisconsin] State Department of Public Instruction developed a program in the 1980's to assist minority and disadvantaged students developing their potential to attend post-secondary institutions. The Early Identification Program (EIP) develops personal relationships with students through counseling on education and academic endeavors, visiting universities and colleges, and assisting with financial aid and post-secondary applications. Figures from the Wausau EIP office show that of the 1996 graduation year, over 80% of the Hmong clients went on to post-secondary schools. Over 90% of the Wausau EIP clients were Southeast Asian. [Researcher

R.] Hutchison's study in The WI Policy Research Institute Report (1997) also stated that the retention rate of Hmong and other Southeast Asian students surpassed that of other groups, including white students. "The rate of increase of Hmong workers is proportional to the rate of their education," [Writes Vang].

Role modeling is another factor that can encourage continued education for Hmong students. Siblings who have attended post-secondary school can attest to the necessities for preparation for a successful education. Many Hmong parents have not acquired education in the US, and few received even elementary education in Laos. Many elders cannot read or write the Hmong language. The pressure for good role models is tremendous. Most females only see women caring for children, the home, and maybe working at a minimum wage employment. It is essential for Hmong college women to become role models for younger girls to help prepare them for college life.

Citizenship Desired but Hard to Achieve

Many Hmong left Laos with intentions of reinforcing militarily and then returning to retake the country from the Pathet Lao [government]. This has not happened, and the young people have only fading memories of the war and their flight. They do not intend to return. These young people feel that the US is their home and officially becoming a US citizen is important. Recent welfare reforms have also threatened those who are not citizens. Many elderly and middle aged Hmong became confused with these government actions. They had been forced to flee Laos because they had aided the US military; now they were being cut off from their only source of income. Many depended upon it to survive.

The House of Representatives, in March of 1997, passed bill H.R. 2202 that would require certification that federal student aid recipients were citizens or permanent legal residents.

The Senate passed a similar bill, S. 1664, that would make legal immigrants ineligible for more than a year of student aid during the first five years in the US. This type of legislation puts pressure on all immigrants who live and work in the US for over five years to make application for citizenship.

To apply for citizenship, a person has to live in the US for 5 years, be over 18, file the necessary papers, and pay over $250 per application and fingerprinting. The process can be very time consuming and requirements have changed numerous times over the last three years. The costs also continue to rise. If the parents become citizens, their children can be processed, but each child has to file a separate application and pay the fees. For a low-income family, this becomes cost prohibitive. There are also trips that need to be taken for interviews with the Immigration and Naturalization Service. If the person passes the examination (covering US history and government), another trip will be necessary for a swearing-in ceremony. The examinations are given in English, and cause difficulty for those who do not have a good understanding of the language. Ten years ago the process was done locally, but changes now make extensive trips necessary.

Myth of the Model Minority May Hurt Young Hmong

[Scholar T.] Otto's (1993) paper on Hmong immigrant students uses the US Census figures to show that Asian/Pacific Islanders have the highest average median income of all minority races. This can be misleading though because many times it is based on family income, with numerous members being employed. Asian students earn the highest scores in math on the SAT [scholastic aptitude test] test. According to Otto, these statistics would make it appear that Asian Americans are the "model minority." This stereotype leads to problems. Asian students are raised in a culture that values the group and prizes politeness. These qualities make them pleasant to work with in the classroom.

The preconceived idea that these students are models may cause them to be given more favorable treatment by teachers. There may even be an inflation of grades simply because the Asian is seen as a "model" student. That can lead to difficulty for the student in a learning environment. When they continue on into a post-secondary institution they may not have the necessary skills to succeed or have to work harder to learn skills that should have been acquired in secondary school.

The Hmong Face Barriers to Getting Jobs

Thomas Moore and Vicky Selkowe

Many American Hmong immigrants are still dependent upon public assistance and welfare many years after their arrival in America. Thomas Moore and Vicky Selkowe did a study of Hmong immigrants in Wisconsin, one of the largest populations of Hmong immigrants in America. In this selection they explain the results of that study and attempt to explain the reasons for this dependence. The authors assert that there are many barriers to work for Hmong immigrants, including a lack of job skills, language difficulties, child care problems, poor health or disability, and transportation. The research supports the claim that most of these immigrants would like to be working instead of relying on public assistance. (The term W-2 used throughout this piece indicates the wage and status of the welfare recipients.)

Moore and Selkowe work for the Institute for Wisconsin's Future. This agency was established in 1994 by a broad coalition of concerned citizens, labor organizations, academics, professionals, religious leaders, and advocacy groups whose goal is to improve living and working conditions of Wisconsin residents. Founding organizations include the Wisconsin State AFL-CIO, the Wisconsin Education Association Council, the Wisconsin Conference of Churches, and the Wisconsin Council on Children and Families.

Despite their disadvantaged position in the job market, the vast majority of Hmong aid recipients want to work. Nearly 72 percent of the respondents [to the authors' survey] answered affirmatively when asked, "Do you want to work?" The 36 respondents who answered "no" were then asked their

Thomas Moore and Vicky Selkowe, "The Impact of Welfare Reform in Wisconsin's Hmong Aid Recipients," *The Institute for Wisconsin's Future*, December 1999, pp. 4–9. Reproduced by permission.

reasons for not wanting to work. Many cited more than one reason, with 18 citing their own poor health, five indicating that they need to care for a sick parent or child, and 17 saying that they are too old to work. Of the 36 respondents who do not want to work, 25 are 50 or more years of age and many have chronic health problems.

Although most of the respondents want to work, they face a number of barriers in seeking or maintaining unsubsidized employment. All respondents were asked about the barriers or problems they have encountered in seeking employment. Their responses are summarized in Table [1] and show that the lack of job skills is most frequently cited as a major obstacle to employment. Nearly half (48.2 percent) feel that their lack of job skills has prevented them from working, while over 40 percent say that their limited ability to speak, read or write English has been an obstacle to employment. In addition, approximately one out of four (24.1 percent) cite child care problems, over 15 percent cite poor health, five percent mention transportation problems, and nearly 10 percent give "other" reasons such as age or having to care for a sick child.

Table 1: Perceived Barriers to Employment

Have any of these problems prevented you from working?	Count	Percent
Lack of job skills	66	48.2%
Language barriers	55	40.1%
Child care problems	37	24.1%
Poor health/disability	21	15.3%
Transportation problems	7	5.1%
Other (age, sick child, etc.)	13	9.5%

Many Hmong Lack Job Skills and Education

The greatest barrier facing these Hmong W-2 participants is their lack of marketable job skills.

The vast majority of Hmong respondents possess few marketable job skills and have very limited work experience. To assess their level of skill preparation, the respondents were presented with the W-2 policy manual's listing of job skills for which training is allowable and asked, "Do you have any of the following skills?"

Approximately 95 percent of respondents indicated that they did not have skills in *any* of these employment areas:

- Basic welding

- Food preparation

- Child care

- Keyboard/data entry

- Electronic assembly

- Utility installation

- Certified nursing assistants

- Press production

- Office software

- Entrepreneurial/small business

- Hospitality training

Only six respondents indicated that they had skills in one of these employment categories, and two stated that they had skills in two of these job areas. The only job skill that a substantial number (13) of respondents reported having was "packing/light assembly," a job category that is not included in the W-2 listing presumably because it does not require even minimal training.

The average education level of Hmong W-2 participants is too low to qualify for even entry level jobs. Literacy levels in both English and Hmong are also extremely low.

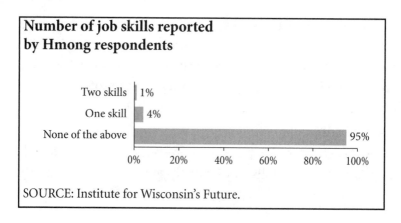

Number of job skills reported by Hmong respondents

Two skills 1%
One skill 4%
None of the above 95%

0% 20% 40% 60% 80% 100%

SOURCE: Institute for Wisconsin's Future.

In addition to their lack of marketable job skills, these Hmong respondents also possess extremely low literacy levels and have a lack of formal education. The average education level of these W-2 participants is quite low, as the chart below demonstrates. More than 60 percent have no formal education, and an additional 30 percent have attended only adult education classes, including classes in English as a Second Language (ESL).

As we might expect given the small number of respondents who have received formal schooling, literacy levels in both English and Hmong are also low. More than 90 percent read little or no English, and over 70 percent have little or no literacy in Hmong.

Hmong Need Assistance to Enter Job Market

Hmong families need a variety of assistance to overcome employment barriers—in particular, they desire technical training.

When Hmong respondents were asked what kinds of assistance they needed to prepare for work, over half (55.5 percent) indicated that they need either technical training, apprenticeships, or more education, while 20 percent say they need classes in English as a Second Language. Although a

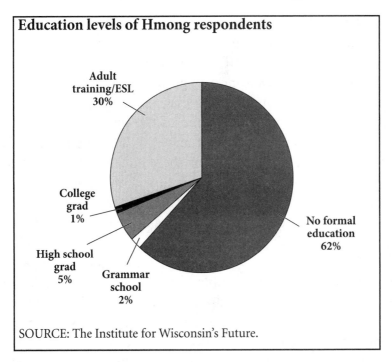

Education levels of Hmong respondents

Adult training/ESL 30%

College grad 1%

High school grad 5%

Grammar school 2%

No formal education 62%

SOURCE: The Institute for Wisconsin's Future.

quarter of all respondents reported that child care problems have prevented them from working, a negligible number (2) feel that they need child care. Many clearly recognize that caring for their children limits their ability to work, yet they appear to be hesitant to place their children in available child care facilities.

Table 2: Assistance Needed to Prepare for Work

What do you need to prepare you to work?	Count	Percent
Technical training	70	51.1%
English as a Second Language courses	28	20.4%
More time	17	12.4%
Apprenticeships	3	2.2%
More education	3	2.2%
Transportation	2	1.5%
Child care	2	1.5%

The survey documents important characteristics of the Hmong families participating in W-2 and the barriers they face in becoming self-sufficient through employment. These primarily middle-aged, non-English speaking refugees have large, two-parent families. The vast majority have no education, minimal literacy and none of the job skills for which training is needed and allowed under W-2. At the same time, the survey reveals that most of these aid recipients want to work, that they perceive their lack of skill training as a major obstacle to employment and that, more than anything else, they want additional technical training to prepare them for the job market.

These findings indicate that the W-2 program, if working effectively, would have ample opportunity to help prepare these families for unsubsidized employment. These Hmong respondents clearly need and desire skill training in the areas that the W-2 policy manual deems important. The W-2 program also allows for basic education (designed primarily to help participants complete a high school equivalency degree) and English as a Second Language courses—both of which would be highly beneficial to these Hmong aid respondents.

Growing Old as a Hmong in America

Kao-Ly Yang

In traditional Hmong society the elderly live with, and are taken care of, by their children, most often their sons. In America the pressures of family and society are changing these old systems of familial care. Many elderly Hmong immigrants are finding themselves living alone, something they never believed would happen to them. In this selection Kao-Ly Yang describes the traditional Hmong customs for caring for the elderly and the challenges Hmong immigrants face in growing old in their modern U.S. communities. Yang also describes the life of many Hmong elderly as they find themselves living longer and in some cases, providing vital services to their families, such as child care.

Yang worked with Hmong elderly health issues with the University of California at San Francisco at the nursing department, then at the Asian Health Program in Fresno.

In the world of change where time and quality request financial independence, what will be the colour of our last age, the old age? Who will take care of us becoming old and disabled? As a worker in a post-industrial society, one only exists by the professional place, the capability to bring back home a salary. As for the Hmong traditional society, one only exists by the social recognition through the kinship and the number of descendants, and not the professional achievement. Reaching the old age, what will be one's life without work, strength to earn a living, family support and love? Beyond the institu-

Kao-Ly Yang, "Hmong Voices: The Elderly Tells Their Stories," during the Interdisciplinary Faculty Development Program on "Cultural Diversity in Health and Aging," at California State University Fresno, Department of Gerontology, June 12–16, 2002, http://www.geocities.com/kaoly_y/archives/TakecareElderly042305.html.

tional protections (the welfare, the Medi-Cal or Medicaid, the retirement), who will be the caring ones that, unfortunately, money cannot pay for?

Hmong people came from far, from a society promoting auto-sufficiency and interdependence to a society in transition where the individualization process develops new forms of solidarity and responsibility among its members: the notion of sufficiency or interdependence concerns more individuals than community growth. Nowadays, what are the duties of a child toward his/her parents? What kinds of expectation do parents have toward their children? In Hmong American communities, what are the needs of elderly people? Are they different in nature if compared to the ones in the traditional settings in Southeast Asia? Is there any gap in term of understanding of the elderly needs, the aging process, the notion of aging on behalf of the children toward their parents and vice versa? Is the senior home becoming the alternative choice for children to take care of their parents? Do elderly parents accept to live in these places?

Awareness of an Emotional Subject

"Grand-mom, why do Hmong people have so many kids?" asked my 8 year-old niece, one day, astonished by the number of brothers and sisters in other Hmong families. In fact, she is a unique [only] child.

"Because when the parents are old, they will have somebody to take care of them", answered my mother, smiling at her grand daughter's curiosity.

"Why don't they just go to the senior houses?" suggested she again.

"Because, in Hmong society, we don't do that", answered the grandmother without explanation, making the little girl feel that there is something not really clear in her grandmother's answer.

"And why?" pursued she.

My mother, tired of her questions, doesn't want to extend the day-long questions of my niece, preferring to continue her embroidery, next to the door-window of our apartment, somewhere in the South of France, where the afternoons are particularly enchanting. As for the little girl, she still wants to know more, preoccupied by her own situation. As she is a unique child, she realized, at the age of 8, that she has to take care, at the same time, of her mother and father now divorced. She wonders after the discussion: "If I have a sister or brother, she or he may take [care] of my dad. I prefer my mom." In the traditional setting, asking such a question wouldn't come out of the mind of a Hmong, especially of a young child. If such a discussion comes out on behalf of children, parents may badly understand the social hidden meanings: they will interpret it as an insult because children would mean they would not want the parents once old. Parents may reply in that case: "Are you thinking to abandon me in some places?" Such a topic has its implied emotional meaning because behind words, there is reason to fear the old age alone.

"Why do we give birth to so many children?" would now ask my mother to her grand daughter if she wants to continue the talk.

And her answer would be:

"Because they will take care of us as we did for them. These are our reasons to live, to love, to give birth, and to raise so many children, to support so many sacrifices, privations and to self-abandon, even to accept to become the member of a new clan, and forever denied by our own birth clan."

Hmong people see life as a successive cycle of steps or rites of passage where each passage leads to a new social status, passing from newborn to child, married-adult/parent then to elderly/grand parent's status. Thus, the notion of "aging" does not only depend on the number of years of life. It basically depends more on the acquirement of the social status at each age. For a man, he becomes an Elderly by passing through the marriage and the acquirement of a name of maturity (*npe laus*). For a woman, she has to pass by the marriage too and the birth of children, especially of a son, to be recognized as an Elderly. Between woman and man, there is however difference in term of permanence of social status: woman will lose all the acquired social prestige if her husband comes to pass away. Both have to have children and grand children, e.g. descendants, to perpetuate the lineage and to care for them, but not only for the old age, but also to honour their soul after death. The physical aspect of aging came, as the last part of defining the aging process. Hmong people identify the aging process by the loss of strength, the loss of memory, the situation of health, visible by chronic illness. But above all these distinctions of becoming old or of being an Elderly, aging is perceived as a social process associated with the acquirement of a social status by effort and commitment in the Hmong culture.

The Traditional Way of Taking Care of the Elderly

All her life, a woman will do farming activities even if she takes of the lighter part. She will lead the domestic work, give birth to children, take good care of them while supporting her husband's lineage. She has to learn during her young age all the necessary assets to later find a good husband. She must be good in embroidering, sewing, cooking, cutting wood, speaking. She must know the social norms and conform all her behaviors to them. She has to behave accordingly to her gender. For a man, he will be in charge of the hardest part of the farming. He will lead the household, play public role towards his clan and other clans, and fulfil rituals duties towards house spirits, ancestors' souls and social events. He, too, has to acquire skills in hunting, seducing and leadership to find a good wife. All the activities for both genders tend to reproduce the group and its values by marriage and giving birth to children, especially sons.

In this patriarchal society, daughters do not directly take care of their parents once married and become members of the allied clan. The responsibilities and duties drop on the sons who have to stay with their parents [when they] become Elderly. The daughters-in-law, considered as new daughters, should love and care [for] the in-laws as their own parents in theory. Even if there is no social prescriptive rule, Hmong parents will always prefer living with the eldest or the youngest son. Daughter with the agreement of her husband will provide material support from time to time during her brief visits.

As caring children, sons will feed, dress and nurse the elderly parents, until their last breath. What I have observed in Laos, a Hmong traditional setting, Elderly, either female or male, could smoke opium and separately eat from the household. If the daughter-in-law is compassionate, the Elderly will find good care: she will wash the Elderly clothes, prepare special food and tender meat in choosing the best pieces for them. But if the opposite situation happens, the Elderly has to do everything by herself or himself. Widowed men would seek to get married again. In the traditional environment, children are *"the only insurance of the old age "* for parents. Indeed, after a life to survive in a hostile environment, by working in monotonous and exhaust[ing] farming tasks, years of living for Hmong Elderly are numbered. There is no precise data on the life expectancy for Hmong Elderly. However, in the United States, only 2.8 % live beyond 64 years old in the census 2000. Even if this percentage is not representative because many Elderly are not American citizens or were not recorded during the census, I think many have died of hardship before reaching the age of Elderly.

Reinforced by the filial pity, daughters, especially sons in this patriarchal society, always feel committed to support their parents until their last days where the sons will accomplish the pitiful funerals for the soul of the dead to find its way back to the village of the ancestors or to the Christian paradise.

Elderly Hmong in Transition

The population of Hmong Elderly over 64 years old is 2.8% according to the census 2000. Currently, there are about 169,428 Hmong in the USA. In 2025, my estimation of the number of Elderly would be about 15% of the total population. As the Hmong community will focus more on the problems of the young generations, Elderly issues may be neglected. According to my opinion, Elderly are like roots that will carry out the youth. There is need to understand Elderly needs and, at the same time, the ones of young people so that there are understanding, social cohesion and coherence in the development of the community.

The transition for the generation of Elderly of 2000 is questioning and promising. Many of them came to the United States as mature adults, henceforth incapable to learn more because of lack of adaptation and also of the necessity to raise a family. Many of them are marked by family trauma and loss, which made them unable to quickly seize new opportunities to build their life in America. The path of war refugees is different on that point with the ones of economic migrants. Hmong people are refugees. They are attached to the past even when they dream or project the future. When reaching the age of 60, whereas their children became autonomous, many of them then have more time for themselves, but discover themselves unprepared to live as individuals. Most of them just face the new age with weariness where they individually felt empty and useless. Some just invested more time in farming, trying to escape loneliness and the lack of exercise that lead to chronic diseases. Others stay at home taking care of their grand children, waiting for better days to travel back home.

Most of Elderly still live with their children while a few have decided to live alone. For the latest, the lack of transportation, of English skills and financial support renders their situation fragile, dependent and emotionally difficult to cope. In Fresno, California, I have observed just a few Hmong Elderly willing to use the public transportation for their everyday needs (most of them are illiterate and incapable to pass the driver licence). This little number is not due to the lack of knowing how to take the bus, but more to the fear of aggression. This means they do live in isolation. As for the Elderly living with their children, most of them are full time babysitters, cooking for the children as well as for the parents who come exhausted from work before taking their children to their own home. There is no time for leisure even if enriching entertaining is rare and culturally non-adapted to Hmong Elderly needs. Wasting money in Casino games just become the bad habit for some, and a source of worry for children, relatives and community leaders.

In the resettlement, there is change. Slowly, there is an acceptance on behalf of Elderly and community towards the idea of living independently from the children. Still, poverty, administrative paperwork, heavy medical treatment, necessary hospitalisation or fear of loneliness, remain barriers for them. Socialized as a member living in interdependence with other members, Hmong Elderly suffers contradiction between living one's life independently and fulfilling the norms and standards.

Shamans in the Hmong American Community

Deborah G. Helsel, Marilyn Mochel, and Robert Bauer

Hmong traditional beliefs about illness often make it difficult for Hmong immigrants to accept the services of the Western medical establishment. Hmong traditional beliefs explain the causes of illness to be soul loss, supernatural events, magical spells, or the expiration of ones "life visa." To address illness, many continue to seek help from Hmong shamans instead of, or in conjunction with, seeking help from American doctors. In this selection the authors explain the role of the traditional shaman and describe how the use of a shaman can help the healing process or contradict the work of medical practitioners. The authors also describe some of the rituals performed by the shamans.

Deborah G. Helsel is a faculty member of the California State University, Fresno. Marilyn Mochel and Robert Bauer are associated with the Healthy House Within a MATCH Coalition, a group in Merced, California, dedicated to improving the health and well-being of all people in their community.

Some biomedical health care providers may not be fully aware or tolerant of traditional healing practices within immigrant communities. Many Hmong Americans, for example, continue to utilize the services of shamans. Physicians and other members of the biomedical health care community may not be comfortable when their patients seek care from shamans and may attempt to impose acceptance of and full patient compliance with biomedical diagnoses and procedures.

Shamans who care for patients in U.S. communities may also feel resentment, disrespect, and frustration for similar

Deborah G. Helsel, Marilyn Mochel and Robert Bauer, "Shamans in a Hmong American Community," *The Journal of Alternative and Complementary Medicine*, vol. 10, 2004, pp. 933–37. Copyright © Mary Ann Liebert, Inc. Reproduced by permission.

reasons. Confused and fearful patients are often caught in the middle of this struggle. In many cases, mutual misunderstanding and disrespect have characterized encounters between Hmong patients, their shamans, and biomedical providers. Mutual awareness and understanding can facilitate a process that ultimately serves the needs of patients and providers....

The traditional culture of immigrant groups is not, of course, simply replaced by that of the new homeland. As [sociologist Wsevolod] Isajiw (1996) noted: "Assimilation has been seen as largely a zero-sum phenomenon, that is, to the extent persons assimilate into dominant society, to that extent they lose their ethnic identity and vice versa, to the extent they retain ethnic identity, to that extent they fail to assimilate." But as our understanding of culture as a dynamic process emerges and grows, so has our awareness that some of the beliefs and practices that have been part of a people's lives for thousands of years persist even as they acculturate. Shamanic healers and rituals are among those that have persisted within the Hmong American community.

Traditional Hmong Beliefs

Traditional Hmong beliefs included several potential sources of illness, including soul loss, supernatural or spirit causes, natural causes, magical causes (spells cast on the afflicted), or the expiration of one's "life visa" or "mandate of life." Health care strategies involved shamanism, herbal medicines, or a combination of the two. Hmong villages always had at least one shaman. Generally, each clan had its own shamans. Sometimes patients would go to a shaman outside their clan, but generally reported feeling more comfortable with the ways of their own clan. Shamans could be male or female, but each had been "chosen" by the spirits to be a shaman. [Ethnographer Jacques] Lemoine (1986) wrote that shamanism was not only taught, it was also inherited; the offspring of a shaman may have inherited the predisposition to become a shaman but then had to be trained by a master shaman for 2 to 3 years or more. New shamans usually learned of their calling through a long and serious illness, which was only cured when the person consented to become a shaman and started training.

Shamans healed their patients by covering their faces with a black cloth and going into a trance so that they could communicate with the spirit world. While in the trance, he or she called out for specific animals to be sacrificed to appease the angry spirits who were responsible for the patient's illness and battled with the forces of evil. An important part of the shaman's work was searching for wandering souls; when the shaman locates and retrieves a lost soul, health is restored. This healing procedure reflects the critical importance of the group in the traditional Hmong culture. The human body is host to several souls; health is restored by restoring the integrity of the group. Shamanic healing restores the connectedness between patient, family and community. At the conclusion of the ceremonies, the shaman was generally offered a meal, paid for his or her services, and given some of the meat from the sacrificed animal to take home. . . .

Studying Shaman Interventions

[In our study] approximately 50% of the shamans interventions were on males; 30% were for females and 20% were listed as a family group. Family contacts were generally made by males on behalf of their families; traditionally, men directed family spiritual events and were responsible for the family's general welfare.

The patients' most frequent complaints included tiredness, weakness, headaches, body aches, loss of appetite, anxiety, and bad dreams. For the most obvious somatic injuries (gunshot wound, broken leg, broken nose, severe bruising) the shamans usually reported that they performed magic healing but the majority of diagnoses involved the effects caused by a wandering soul, lost soul, sad soul, evil spirits or of a "life visa" that was expiring and needed extension by the patients' ancestors.

Shamans Work with the Soul

Many shamans described the patients as not having intact souls, noting that they needed to be restored. Souls had wandered off and needed to find their way back to the body for health to be restored. One shaman noted that his patient had "witnessed a car accident that involved a death, so his soul had wandered." In some cases, the shamans would suggest building a "soul bridge" to show the soul the way home; other times they would simply call the soul back. Strings around the wrist, ankle or neck, metal bracelets, anklets or neck rings, or even safety pins on clothing may be used to secure the soul.

Sometimes the souls of ancestors were communicating displeasure and needed a feast or other action taken by those in the land of the living to quiet the restlessness that was resulting in the patient's illness. In one instance, the ancestor missed being worshipped regularly. In another case, the deceased father did not want his son to take the clan name of his widow's new husband; the son's neck pain went away as soon as his father's soul was promised that would not happen. One man's illness was interpreted to be the direct result of his deceased wife trying to take his soul away to join her. The eye pain of another patient had been caused, the shaman wrote, because he had converted to Christianity and offended several ancestors. Another patient was having trouble with headaches and fainting because, his shaman wrote, he had promised his ancestors a feast but had failed to provide it.

Some patients sought shamanic healing, they reported, because their physician was unable to diagnose their problem: "Patient is ill: doctor can't diagnose"; "Unexplainable illness that doctor doesn't know what is going on." In some of these cases of unexplained, prolonged illness, the shamans predicted that the patient "could become a shaman in the future." In other cases, the shamans' patients listed their biomedical diagnoses or condition as their complaints: "dialysis patient"; "stroke"; "diabetes and urinary tract infection (UTI)"; "asthma and diabetes." For these patients, involved shamans sometimes diagnosed a spiritual problem for which they suggested a healing while in other instances they said that there was no spiritual problem with which they could help.

Sometimes Shamans Could Not Help

There were also other instances wherein the shaman did not feel the problem was within his or her area of expertise. In one case, the shaman described the patient's complaint of a sore throat but said he could "see no problem spiritually." In other instances, the shamans felt it was too late to intervene. One said that the soul of the patient (diagnosed with a stroke by a physician) was lost, and it was too late to chase and catch his soul. Another simply noted that the patient's "life visa" had already expired.

Diagnoses in a few cases eloquently expressed the enormous impact of recent Hmong historical events on the shaman's beliefs and practices. In one case a bird had flown into the home of a shaman's family indicating to him that there was war in the ancestor's world; this, he warned, could be both prolonged and devastating for those in both worlds. In another case, the shaman concluded that the patient had suffered foot pain for more than 2 years because someone had destroyed the grave of his grandfather in Laos.

There were many examples of using shamanic care for prophylaxis. The annual curing ceremonies for families, soul calling, and naming ceremonies for infants or ceremonies prior to and after hospitalization for surgery are examples of such prophylaxis. Pregnant women go to shamans for "soul-splitting" ceremonies so that their souls and the souls of their unborn children are separate and, if one dies, the other will live. In one case, the shaman noted that the patient came to him because she was "getting old" and "requesting a visa extension."

In these data, we also saw evidence of the emergence of new shamans. Shamans, as noted earlier, generally learn of their calling during a long illness, and several patient contacts noted that "the patient will be a shaman" or "the spirits have chosen him to be a shaman." Once this diagnosis was made, these individuals entered training with an older, more experienced master shaman to begin the process of training under his/her guidance.

It was of interest that the shamans generally used the term "soul" in reference to the noncorporeal parts of humans (patients or ancestors) but used the word "spirit" in reference to the nonhuman parts of various locations or items. In this data, that included house spirits, fireplace spirits, spirits of the city of Merced, and even a world spirit. While souls could be lost, spirits generally needed appeasing with sacrifices. One female patient presented with neck pain; the shaman asked if she had caused an animal suffering by hurting its neck. She indicated that she had twisted the neck of a rat; the animal's spirit was causing her pain. In another case, the world spirit was causing a patient to become violent. Another woman had a "sickness the doctor can't diagnose"; the shaman concluded her problem was evil spirits. One respondent came to the shaman because a snake had entered her house; the shaman noted that her ancestors were trying to warn her that an evil spirit had entered her house. The Hmong believe that the ancestral world, the human world, and the spiritual world, while distinct, overlap.

Hmong Won't Reject Traditions

Ethnographers [Dwight] Conquergood and [P.] Thao (1989) wrote that it is a misconception to presume that individuals from diverse ethnic and cultural backgrounds will, once they encounter biomedicine, simply reject the traditional health practices that have served them for centuries. A 1997 study of Hmong healing practices in the San Joaquin Valley by [P.] Nuttal and [R.] Flores confirmed that the Hmong were more likely to use shamanism, herbal medicine, or talismans than biomedical health care providers and, in fact, only used bio-medicine as a last resort [G.] Plotnikoff [and others] (2002) from the University of Minnesota described shamanism in the large Hmong population in Minnesota and noted that "many Hmong who see physicians also rely on shamans for restoring health and balance to their body and soul."

In his work on ethnicity and health care, [Pao] Lee noted that in some cases, as members of ethnic communities be-come more familiar with biomedical care, they become disil-lusioned when their expectations are not met. Some of the shamans' patients' complaints in our data included references to conditions that physicians had not been able to diagnose or cure. Some of these, as noted earlier, involved chronic ill-nesses. The management of diabetes, hypertension and other chronic conditions does not seem to be well understood by many Hmong Americans. The idea of medical control or maintenance has not historically been one with which they were familiar; one is either sick or not. If one is sick, and if one finds the right shaman, s/he will be healed.

Traditionally, several health care strategies were utilized si-multaneously or sequentially. [Researchers] Paul and Elaine Lewis (1984), describing tribal life in Southeast Asia, wrote in *Peoples of the Golden Triangle,*

> In their quest for health, Hmong do not become discour-aged if one ritual does not result in a cure, but try one after another until the right one is found.... Curing is not lim-ited to such ceremonies. Many Hmong men and women have a knowledge of herbal medicines widely used for com-mon ailments. Increasingly they are also turning to modern

medicine. In many cases they first perform ritual healing ceremonies, then seek the help of modern medical practitioners.

This plan of action closely resembles concurrent utilization by patients in the general population of complementary and alternative medical providers along with biomedical providers; [W.] Cockerham (2004) notes that "the majority of patients who use chiropractic services do not depend entirely on this method of care . . . they use chiropractors and physicians in a complementary manner." Many of the Hmong American patients in our study appeared to use shamans and physicians in this way.

Integrating Shamans with Western Medicine

Jacques Lemoine (1986) described the traditional obligation of the Hmong shaman to help patients "recover psychic balance" or "restore the self." This was done in the framework of the familiar shamanic rituals that clarified the links between the worlds of humans, ancestors and spirits. The need for these services, he noted, certainly persisted amid the stresses, fears and uncertainties that accompanied the Hmong's arrival in their new homeland. In such a setting, he wrote, the shaman was not competing with the medical doctor but providing an alternative form of care that could complement biomedicine.

The Hmong American community continues to experience the effects of their geographic and cultural displacement. Hmong Americans, for example, are at an increased risk for noninsulin dependent diabetes mellitus (NIDDM) and complications including hypertension and renal failure. [P.] Freund [and others] (2003) noted that a combination of factors in the way of life in industrialized countries may be implicated in the disease since groups immigrating into industrialized societies from agricultural communities are at increased risk for NIDDM. [J.] Scheder (1988) asserted that increased rates of NIDDM are also found in groups with high levels of stress, disrupted social networks, social marginality, feelings of hopelessness and helplessness, and poverty. Virtually every aspect of Hmong lives has been disrupted; the task of helping them restore and maintain health may well be best served by the contributions of both shamanic care and biomedicine.

Now, almost three decades since they began arriving in the United States, Hmong Americans continue to craft and recraft a culture-in-transition. There are, of course, as many health care options within the Hmong American culture as there are in the general population; Hmong patients in Merced [California], for example, can seek the services of a number of care providers, including a Hmong American physician and/or shamans as well as a number of other complementary and alternative medical providers. As noted earlier, acculturation is not a zero-sum phenomenon; some traditional beliefs and practices may persist even as a group acquires others. Hmong immigrants from a traditionally familistic and group-oriented culture have become part of a culture described by [R.] Bellah [and others] (1985) as individualistic and competitive. But as Conquergood and Thao noted, the Hmong world view perceived of a "sick society" as being one that is highly individualistic. In their recently adopted homeland, Hmong Americans may feel the need to seek out shamans to restore the sense of connection into their group, their culture and their family that helps them feel whole and healthy. Decreasing these patients' sense of isolation through familiar, communal shamanic activities may help to achieve the elusive comfort that they seek. This connectedness may also serve to ease the sadness of some of the losses they have sustained as a group and as individuals. The "restless spirits" of dead parents, spouses, and children left behind in Laos were frequently identified by shamans as sources of illness; this interpretation may be part of a cultural expression of the pain of their losses and their ongoing uncertainty that coming to America was the best thing for them, their families and their culture. Many Hmong Americans apparently share the sentiments expressed by one who noted: "Laos still remains, deep inside me."

Many Hmong Reject Western Psychiatry

Kaomi Goetz

The Hmong language does not have a word for mental illness. Traditionally, the Hmong believe that only a shaman can help restore health to a suffering person by restoring that person's spirit. This belief makes it difficult for Hmong to get needed help from the medical community until a mental illness is so advanced it becomes more than just a daily inconvenience. In this selection Kaomi Goetz reports on this dilemma and how the desire to seek the help of shamans first harms not just the patient, but the larger Hmong community. By not getting needed help early, otherwise vibrant members of the community are unable to participate fully because of debilitating difficulties such as depression, isolation, and loneliness. Since nearly all first-generation immigrants lost relatives in the Vietnam War, these symptoms of grief are prevalent within the entire community.

Goetz is a journalist for Minnesota Public Radio.

There is no word for mental illness in the Hmong language. What western science knows as mental illness, traditional Hmong religion Ua Dab says is a sign of an evil or unhappy spirit. When an evil spirit takes over the body of a person, a shaman is called in to appease or drive out the spirits.

Incense fills the air of a living room in St. Paul [Minnesota] where 10 relatives of a 17-year-old girl have gathered. The girl is suffering hallucinations. The family believes she has been taken over by the Spirit of Death and may soon die. A Hmong shaman wears a black hood and clutches hand cymbals. He gyrates and chants before the group. A slaughtered pig is offered as a sacrifice to the evil spirit. A goat, representing the seriousness of the illness, was sacrificed earlier.

Chanting in Hmong, the shaman says he's traveling on horseback into the spirit world to reclaim the spirits of the young woman. The shaman warns the evil spirits he is ready to do battle. He stomps his feet to get their attention. The chanting could last for hours.

Following the ceremony, the family will eat a meal consisting of the sacrificial meat and by doing so, believe they will eat away the evil.

If First Shaman Fails, Go to Another

Since this ritual, her father reports his daughter has been cured. But if the hallucinations return, the family will likely not turn to a doctor, but instead try another shaman. Hmong leaders say while not all immigrants utilize shamans, the practice is still used by the majority of Hmong living in Minnesota to address both physical and mental ailments.

"Right now, the very first step is getting the community to acknowledge they have mental illness," says Mee Vang, executive director of Hmong United International Council. The council represents the state's nearly 42,000 Hmong. Vang says the group encourages Hmong to seek out western doctors for treatment of mental illness. But Vang says western medicine is still not widely accepted.

"A lot of people are still adjusting, that there's other explanations on why someone is sick—not just the soul. Things that the shamanistic rituals can't explain anymore," says Vang.

Dr. Paul Reitman, a forensic psychologist at Fairview University Hospital, says his Hmong patients often wait until late stages of an illness before seeking help.

"I don't believe the Hmong community accepts psychiatry as Western culture," says Reitman. "The average person in America might consider that psychiatric care has a place. I think people in the Hmong community will not acknowledge symptoms as symptoms of a mental illness. Instead they'll look at their symptoms representing a physical ailment, or they might even think of it as demons."

Mental Health Care May Be a Last Resort

Reitman says many of his patients come to him only after the shaman has failed to cure them. And he says his Hmong patients will often stop taking prescribed medicine if they believe they're cured. Not understanding the concept of ongoing or preventative treatment can result in tragedy, as in the case of Mee Xiong. Relatives say she had consulted a shaman to cast out the evil spirit. According to court records, Xiong had also seen a Minnesota psychiatrist for the past four years, and was under court order to take medication. Reitman says Hmong people are no more prone to violence or mental illness than people from other cultures.

Ilean Her of the Council of Asian Pacific Minnesotans, and others in the Hmong community, insist these shaman rituals work in some circumstances. But she admits shamanism can't cure everything. And shamans are not known to recommend a western doctor. She says such sole adherence to shamanism can have negative consequences.

"I have a friend who teaches in Minneapolis public schools and she has a child with a learning disability. She told the parents, and they say 'Oh no, we go to a shaman to fix it or through traditional Hmong medicine to fix it.' In two or three years the learning disability has gotten worse because the intervention hasn't been given to him," says Her. "It's a detriment to the community. I'm not saying shamanism doesn't work, but at the same time, there are certain conditions if you are not treated right away, your condition becomes worse."

Her says by coming to the U.S. and jumping 200 years into the technological future from their hill tribe way of life, the Hmong face tremendous stress. Some 35,000 Hmong were killed aiding U.S. forces during the war in Southeast Asia, a high percentage of their overall population. This means nearly every Hmong immigrant in Minnesota lost a friend or relative due to the war. She says turning to a shaman is one way to maintain a link to their traditional culture.

"Depression, loneliness, isolation, particularly of the older generation, where they feel they don't fit in, they don't belong, they miss home, they miss their country, they miss their food, and then it becomes more complex," Her says. "The experience of coming to America, acculturation, is an additional stress on pre-existing mental illness within the community. It intensifies depression, it intensifies paranoia, and they don't have a basis to understand that."

Health care providers are discovering ways to reach Hmong acceptance by blending their practices with shaman understanding. A Wilder program is staffed by Hmong and educates about mental illness using Hmong language materials. A St. Paul Hmong women's support group and an elders drop-in center in Minneapolis offer help to combat isolation, family problems and cultural adjustments.

The Hmongs' Success in Minnesota

Stephen Magagnini

The two largest communities of Hmong immigrants in America are in Minnesota and California. However, the Hmong in Minnesota have assimilated into American culture faster and have become much more prosperous than their California cousins. In this selection Stephen Magagnini explains the factors that contribute to the Hmongs' greater success in Minnesota, including differences in climate, the number of other immigrant minorities, and the basic costs of living in each state. The biggest reason for the difference, Magagnini argues, is the nature of the outreach provided to Hmong families in the two communities. In Minnesota, religious and other social organizations provided substantial one-on-one aid to the Hmong immigrants, whereas in California most of the immigrants had only the government bureaucracies to help them.

Magagnini is an investigative reporter for the Sacramento Bee.

M any of the 16,000 Hmong refugees coming to America from Thailand this year [2004] must decide whether to join their relatives in Minnesota, or those in California. And, despite subzero winters and mosquito-infested summers, a growing number are choosing Minnesota. They're not the only ones. Enterprising, well-educated young Hmong from Sacramento to Providence, R.I., are flocking to be part of the Minnesota Hmong miracle.

Although California still has more Hmong than Minnesota—an estimated 95,000 compared to around 70,000—Minnesota Hmong rule in every conceivable area: income, education, politics and business.

Stephen Magagnini, "Special Report: The Leftover People," *Sacramento Bee*, September 12, 2004. Reproduced by permission.

Their amazing leap from St. Paul's Frogtown ghetto—where most began life in America as illiterate tribespeople—to positions of influence and affluence can be traced to an economic and social climate more hospitable than what Hmong found in California. The Minnesota Hmong have tasted more success, in large part because church sponsors, foundations, educators, employers, lenders and public officials pitched in from the start to speed the Hmong on the road to self-sufficiency.

"The mainstream community opened their hearts to the Hmong," said Xang Vang, who arrived in Minnesota in the winter of 1977 lonely, homesick and unemployed. Today, Vang, 54, makes a nice living buying and renovating homes.

Minnesota Hmong are more than three times as likely to own their own homes as those in California, their median family income is more than $12,000 higher per year, and they are more likely to finish high school and college.

Hmong Community in Minnesota

St. Paul—now the nation's largest Hmong metropolis with more than 40,000—has become the Hmong Paris, home to Hmong comedians, playwrights, artists and filmmakers.

Hmong Americans can be found at every level of government from the St. Paul school board to the state Senate, where a Hmong woman is the majority whip. The only Hmong elected officials in California are school board members, even though Sacramento has about 25,000 Hmong and Fresno, 35,000.

At the end of February [2003], in a testament to Hmong clout in Minnesota, St. Paul Mayor Randy Kelly led a 19-person delegation—including seven Hmong professionals—to Thailand to welcome the 16,000 refugees to America and to evaluate their educational and medical needs.

Meanwhile, Sacramento Mayor Heather Fargo said she didn't realize a new wave of Hmong was coming until a May

29 meeting with local Asian American leaders. Fargo said no Hmong had contacted her, and she wasn't aware that there was a Sacramento Hmong refugee task force, although she's since formed a task force of her own.

In the Sacramento area, Hmong compete for services with more than 50 other ethnic groups, including the more numerous Latinos and the Russian-speaking refugees, as well as Iu Mien tribespeople from Laos, Bosnians and others. In contrast, St. Paul's Hmong are the city's largest immigrant group.

Hmong Thrive in a Competitive Atmosphere

Along with Minnesota's generally more welcoming climate, there's a local drive to be the best that has rubbed off on the Hmong, said Sia Lo, the mayor's senior policy adviser.

"You see it between Medtronic and St. Jude Medical (medical technology companies), between 3M and Honeywell," Lo said. "It's in that healthy spirit of competition that the Hmong are thriving."

The Twin Cities—St. Paul and Minneapolis—boast two Hmong newspapers, two Hmong cultural centers, three Hmong-owned Best Steakhouses and even a Hmong-Latino nightclub with two dance floors, one for Hmong hip-hop, the other for salsa. The 175-member Minnesota Hmong Chamber of Commerce sponsors its own golf tournament; there is no California Hmong chamber.

The St. Paul area has 18 Hmong lawyers and five Hmong medical clinics; Sacramento has one of each. St. Paul has more than 500 Hmong real estate agents; Sacramento has fewer than 50. The St. Paul Police Department has 13 Hmong officers; the Sacramento department has one.

The most stunning symbol of the Minnesota Hmong's upward mobility is Cedarhurst—a 26-room Civil War-era mansion on the outskirts of St. Paul—that's now home to a Hmong doctor and his family.

St. Paul has become the standard for Hmong success worldwide, said real estate developer Cha Vang, son of the famous Hmong war hero, Gen. Vang Pao, who lives in Orange County. "We came from the mountains, we didn't know how to read and write, and now we run multimillion-dollar companies and make huge investment decisions," Vang said.

Initial Hostility in Minnesota

The Hmong in Minnesota and California started even: in the ghettoes of Sacramento, Fresno and St. Paul—cities where refugee resettlement agencies had found sponsors for them.

"People tried to burn our house down three times in two years," recalls Tou Ger Xiong, a Hmong comedian who was 6 years old when his family moved from Thailand to the Frogtown ghetto in 1980. "We had our windows cracked 32 times. My dad would take his battery out of the car and store it inside. My mom didn't want to walk from the house to the bus stop."

Hmong families desperate for work drifted to Minnesota anyway. Like the Hmong in Fresno and Sacramento, they faced their share of insensitivity. Yee Chang, a St. Paul Realtor, said that in the 1980s he and other Hmong teens learned martial arts to defend themselves from assaults. Even in college at St. Olaf's south of Minneapolis, Chang said some of his classmates joked about watching their pets around him, implying the Hmong ate dogs.

While many Hmong got lost in California—which had already attracted thousands of other Asian and Latino immigrants—they immediately stood out in Minnesota, which was 97 percent white. "People were kind of enchanted by them," said Jane Kretzmann, who worked for Lutheran Social Service, one of the largest resettlement agencies.

The first Hmong had barely arrived when the Governor's Office called Kretzmann asking her to hire a bilingual Hmong worker because another 150 refugees were coming. St. Paul

Mayor George Latimer got police and health officials to em-
ploy Hmong interpreters, and in his 1978 State of the City
speech, he welcomed the Hmong to town. Latimer said he
didn't have to "run around and convince people the Hmong
had a right to be here. That was a given."

Church Groups Provide Essential Aid

Sacramento County Executive Terry Schutten—who lived in
St. Paul from 1986 to 1999, serving as the Ramsey County
manager—said local church groups virtually adopted the
Hmong.

"Our parish had programs where we would go and work
with a Hmong family," he said. "My wife and kids took over
furniture and mattresses and tables, and at Christmas there
was a huge drive, presents and food, and then we delivered
the gifts. There's a lot more of a sense of pulling together to
help the newcomers."

Lutherans, Catholics and Presbyterians took in refugees or
found them housing. They organized summer programs and
English classes, and encouraged the Hmong to buy starter
homes as soon as possible, then trade up. Sometimes, the
sponsors actually helped make a down payment, Kretzmann
said.

May Ying Ly, a Sacramento Hmong leader, said the Minnesota family that sponsored her nephew's wife put her in
their will: "She's like their own daughter."

Ly's family also had loving sponsors, a doctor and his wife.
But they lived in Hawaii, and Ly's family migrated on to Cali-
fornia in the late 1970s, along with thousands of other
Hmong.

California Seemed Like Paradise

Initially, California—not Minnesota—promised to be the
Hmong paradise in America, a place they could farm year
round. Their political leader, Gen. Vang Pao, had settled in

Southern California, declaring Minnesota too cold for his aging bones. And California welfare payments were higher, a draw for mostly illiterate refugees without marketable skills.

But reality fell far short of that promise. Families that did get farm work harvested crops from 5 a.m. to 9 p.m., often with their children, leaving little time for homework. And the Hmong faced heavy competition for fieldwork and other entry-level jobs from Latinos, Filipinos and other immigrants.

Those Hmong who landed first in California often were sponsored by immigrants still learning the system themselves. Robert Khang, the first Hmong to arrive in Sacramento, said his sponsors—a Vietnamese family—took his wife and year-old son home for dinner on their first night in the United States, then checked them into a motel on Stockton Boulevard.

"After two weeks, they said they could not help me any more," Khang said. "My son was very sick with pneumonia, but the sponsor did not take him to the hospital. We had only one meal a day, and I couldn't communicate. I cried every day."

In the early 1990s, California's higher home prices continued to rise, and unemployment topped 8 percent.

Industrial Work Proves Better than Farm Work

Meanwhile, Minnesota's economy—built on 350,000 manufacturing jobs—took off. By 1998, unemployment had fallen to 2.4 percent, half the national average, and "anyone who wanted a job got one," said Minnesota demographer Barbara Ronningen.

By decade's end, an estimated 8,000 California Hmong had moved to Minnesota. From the beginning, Minnesota's charitable foundations teamed up with public officials and vocational colleges to train thousands of Hmong for $15-an-hour assembly line work.

The jobs required little English, but good hand-eye coordination—a skill Hmong women had developed over years of stitching *pa ndao*, the colorful needlework for which the Hmong are famous. Others were trained as nursing assistants, machinists, welders and computer operators.

Local Hmong organizations made sure the trainees succeeded. "If somebody didn't show up for work, somebody from the staff of the Hmong organizations would go work their shift," said Kretzmann.

Hmong who were picking cucumbers in Minnesota 20 years ago now make everything from airline meals to heart valves. Those jobs have turned the Hmong into taxpayers and helped them buy houses and, in many cases, establish a family routine: At least one parent gets home in time to make sure the kids do their homework.

Schools Are Better in Minnesota

Minnesota's public schools—among the nation's best, with much higher high school graduation rates and math, science and reading scores than California—also have nurtured the Hmong renaissance.

By 1980, the St. Paul School District had joined forces with the city and county to hire Hmong teachers and counselors to propel the Hmong forward, said Sacramento County Executive Schutten, who previously held a similar job in St. Paul. "That whole sense of cooperation to get the job done is critical and it's frankly more advanced than it is here (in Sacramento)."

In 1983, Yang Dao, the first Hmong refugee to receive a doctorate, resettled in St. Paul. Yang told the Minnesota Hmong their future was in America, not Laos, and preached education as a panacea for poverty. Yang's daughter-in-law, Kou Her, 28, attended ninth grade in Sacramento before her family moved to St. Paul.

In Sacramento, she said, "It was hard to get out of ESL (English as a Second Language) class—I told the teacher I felt like I was wasting my time. When I got to St. Paul, ESL was gone. The school was better, the teachers were better, and I got more attention."

It helps that Hmong have served on the St. Paul school board since 1992. A few months ago, board member Kazoua Kong-Thao got a call from a Hmong dad whose daughter had failed a reading test required for graduation and was threatening to kill herself. "I got her a tutor through the school and she passed on her final try," Kong-Thao said.

Success Breeds More Success in Minnesota

Success breeds success. Though some Hmong kids were bullied in school, many of those born in Laos adopted their parents' work ethic and rose to the top of their classes anyway, much as many Vietnamese kids have done in Sacramento.

Comedian Xiong became valedictorian of his class and won a scholarship to Carleton College, south of Minneapolis. Now 30, he lives in a four-bedroom house in the tony St. Paul suburb of Woodbury, and confers daily with his financial planner—who's also Hmong.

He makes as much as $6,000 a speech as a motivational speaker for corporate America, but he's always doing free, spontaneous performances in Hmong neighborhoods. At the Hope Academy Hmong charter school recently, he delighted a class of sixth-graders with his dead-on imitation of a Hmong teenage girl with attitude, then told them to be proud they live in two worlds.

Xiong and other young Hmong constantly travel between those worlds. On a recent Saturday, at a shaman ceremony for his uncle's new daughter, Xiong dined with 30 other males while the women waited their turn. That night, he and his East Indian fiancee feasted at Tango Sushi, run by four Hmong brothers, then partied at Club Escape, a hot Twin Cities nightspot. "It's a great time to be Hmong—this is where the action is," said Xiong over a beer at Malina's, a sports bar run by two Hmong social workers.

He recalled the days when University Avenue, the main drag in Frogtown, was a gantlet of strip joints, drug dealers, gang-bangers and hookers. Today it's the Hmong Champs-Elysees, lined with pastry shops, bookstores, newspaper offices and restaurants. "Frogtown has pretty much become Hmong-town," Xiong says. "We're taking over slowly. We don't have a Don Corleone, but we have a friend of a friend of a friend."

Success Doesn't Come Easy in California

One of those friends telephoned Fresno supermarket owner Cha Fong Lee and his son-in-law Dan Vang in 1999 with an offer they couldn't refuse.

The friend connected them with a Hmong officer at Western Bank in St. Paul, which loaned them $3 million to buy a dying mall in Brooklyn Center, a western suburb of Minneapolis. "It was the eyesore of Brooklyn Center, only 40 percent occupied," Vang said. "We took it over and anchored it and now it's 75 percent rented.

"The most critical piece was they had a Hmong person making this decision; the gatekeepers actually lent an ear to somebody who knew the ins and outs of the community."

In Fresno, which had no Hmong bankers, Vang said it took them six years to qualify for a business loan. "There was a lot of ignorance on both sides," he said. "They didn't know what the Hmong community is, and we didn't fit the normal credit (profile): a large amount of assets, a certain amount of cash flow, been in business for X amount of years. The Hmong have been in America for 25 years, but we've really only done business for the last 10."

Vang now lives in a Minneapolis suburb with his wife and two small daughters. He hates the cold but loves the atmosphere: "There's a willingness of the general community to embrace us. Around here they call it the Minnesota Nice: 'We'll welcome you as long as you succeed.'"

Hmong Prove to Be a Good Risk for Banks

Lao Lu Hang, a Hmong loan officer with Western Bank, says the Hmong gamble hasn't turned out to be a gamble at all: Fewer than 10 percent of the bank's 200 or so Hmong business customers have defaulted—far below the national average.

Hmong repay their loans because the culture demands it, Hang said. To owe money is shameful and all debts must be settled before you die. Today, Minnesota's Hmong get business loans at the same rate as non-Hmong, according to the Federal Reserve.

Some problems remain. Not every Minnesota Hmong is a success story. Police count more than a dozen violent Hmong gangs, including a few, such as the Oroville Mono Boys, filled with California transplants.

About a quarter of Minnesota's Hmong, many of them elderly and disabled, remain on public assistance. So many Hmong have been placed in public housing projects that Ramsey County was recently sued—unsuccessfully—for favoring the Hmong over other ethnic groups.

There is a growing class gap between the new Hmong intelligentsia and older, more traditional Hmong, some of whom fear assimilation is coming at the expense of Hmong culture. But there are signs of accommodation:

A Hmong driving school teaches Hmong elders who don't speak English how to drive. More than 100 Hmong women have been certified as day-care providers, and now run a co-op. A grass-roots group, Hmong Men for Peace and Unity, has taken on the long-taboo topics of domestic violence and gender roles. . . .

Hmong in Thailand Are Sold on Life in Minnesota

St. Paul Mayor Kelly's fact-finding delegation to the Hmong camp in Thailand in February [2003] inadvertently sold thousands of Hmong on Minnesota. A few Hmong even assumed Kelly was running for president.

Before Kelly's trip, about 8,000 of the camp-dwellers were leaning toward California; now they're evenly divided, with each state expecting about 5,500 refugees, according to State Department estimates. The rest will go mostly to Wisconsin, North Carolina and other states with Hmong enclaves ready to sponsor them.

The new Hmong—who began arriving in late June—already are getting the "Minnesota Nice" treatment. More than 4,000 families, Hmong and non-Hmong alike, have volunteered to help them. St. Paul has contracted with Hmong organizations to provide job training and English classes. The health department has added eight bilingual staff members.

Sacramento County health officials have hired five bilingual staff members, but the county—which has one of the highest concentrations of refugees in America—plans to rely largely on existing programs.

"We've been resettling refugees since the 1980s," said Sacramento County refugee coordinator Roy Kim. "We have an existing structure in place that doesn't need to be built up or built out."

Sacramento County school officials plan to put the newcomers directly into ESL classes in regular schools. In St. Paul, the school district has created four transitional schools where new Hmong children will go for six months before they're eased into regular schools.

Minnesotans "have a social compact, a history and a culture of all of us working together," Kelly said, to ensure that the Hmong—like the French Canadians, Germans, Irish and Scandinavians before them—become productive citizens as quickly as possible.

Hmong Farm Enterprises in America

Spencer Sherman

For thousands of years, the Hmong were a tribal people whose subsistence was dependent upon a style of farming called slash-and-burn. The slash-and-burn style of farming consists of culti-vating a patch of land, strip it of its resources, burn what is left and move to a new patch of land. It suited a nomadic tribe's way of life for thousands of years. In America, however, slash-and-burn is not only inefficient and environmentally disastrous, it is also illegal. The Hiawatha Valley Farm Project was born, a one-year experimental offshoot of the Highland Lao Initiative, a federally funded initiative aimed at bolstering social services in communities that were losing Hmong residents. The project's goal was to help address the lack of understanding Hmong im-migrant farmers had of modern farming. This California project helped these farmers get land and learn the farming techniques that would bring success to them in this new land. In this selec-tion Spencer Sherman describes the difficulties arising from the lack of modern skills and how the project helped many Hmong find new independence.

Sherman is a former Supreme Court correspondent and re-porter for the United Press International. In 1985 he won a fel-lowship with the Alicia Patterson Foundation for excellence in his reporting on the struggle of the Hmong in America.

It is shortly after dark as the headlights on Dang Moua's van sweep across a wide stretch of farmland north of Merced [California]. The lights fall on an irrigation ditch as the van drops into a muddy puddle, then the beams come to rest on a

Spencer Sherman, "Charting a Course to the American Dream," http://www.aliciapatterson.org?APF_Reporter/Index.html#S, 1985. Reproduced by permis-sion. This article was prepared by Spencer Sherman under a grant from the Alicia Patterson Journalism Foundation.

low sheet-metal building as the vehicle rolls to a stop. Inside, a chorus of primitive grunts echo into the night. Dang Moua motions for everyone in the van to remain seated. Everything goes black as he shuts off the lights and walks into the building. Suddenly it is swathed in light and the grunting reaches a feverish pitch. Dang Moua motions towards the building and, inside, hundreds of hogs race towards him, stumbling over each other to reach the feeding bins.

Dang Moua moved to the San Joaquin Valley in 1979, one of the first Hmong refugees to do so. He had saved some money and used it as a down-payment on a farm, where he built a barn and slaughtering room and started a hog farm, knowing that other Hmong coming into the valley would need his product because their diet is heavy on pork. His predictions were correct and now, "I have a bigger market for the pigs than I can supply," he said.

His logic is simple and clear, and in keeping with the thinking of immigrants who have come before him. He used knowledge brought from Laos to provide a service to his fellow refugees. He learned a few hard lessons along the way about financing, agriculture and marketing. In one instance, after he poured the concrete slab for the slaughtering house, the building inspector told him to rip it up because he had not reinforced the floor with steel.

"You know, back home, we butcher a pig outside on the ground," he said, "Here you have health inspectors, building codes, many problems."

Hmong Skills Were Not Appropriate in America

The greatest problem is that most Hmong skills are not appropriate in the American economy. In Laos they were simple farmers who would burn a section of jungle and let the ashes nourish rice, vegetables and their cash crop, opium. This type of agriculture—called "slash and burn"—is simple, but inefficient, environmentally disastrous, and illegal in the United States.

Dang Moua's experience has been repeated across the country. But like his experience, many of the projects begin in fits and starts, each a learning experience in the American way.

Unlike many Vietnamese refugees who came to the United States as skilled businessmen, doctors, teachers and fishermen, the Hmong had no experience in business. The first attempts at economic development for most Hmong in their 30s and 40s came when they arrived in the United States after a decade of full-time soldiering in Laos. The concept of self-improvement for Hmong in the hills of Laos meant growing more food on free land, breeding healthy hogs and harvesting larger crops of powerful opium.

"There is something fundamental that I have found working with the Hmong. That is that they must go through (a project) once, then they can do it themselves," says Jane Kretzmann, the state refugee coordinator for Minnesota, where 10,000 Hmong live, largely in the twin cities of Minneapolis and St. Paul.

Patronizing Attitudes Don't Help the Problem

But, she admits, often the fault lies with Americans who bring patronizing feelings along with an honest desire to help. "In working with the Hmong, we Americans always try to do it our way. The Hmong way has to be the second time around," Kretzmann lamented recently.

But before 1983, the vast majority of Hmong did not know how to do it themselves, even when it came to getting an entry level job as a janitor or maid.

In February, 1993, Dang Moua and other Hmong leaders from around the country were brought to Washington, DC, to meet with federal officials and representatives from private industry to search for answers to this Hmong economic quagmire.

No one thought the Washington meeting would be the start of something big; they were looking for the start of something small. But the meeting signaled a growing awareness of the intractable resettlement problems of the Hmong. The meeting was organized by the Indochinese Resource Action Committee and Carol Leviton, the seemingly tireless projects coordinator for the Hmong/Highlander Development Fund, a private loan guarantee fund for Hmong development.

"I think the government looked at the meeting as bringing together the 'Indian Chiefs' to tell them it was time for them to get going on their own," says Leviton, one of a small cadre of former Peace Corps volunteers and U.S. government employees in Thailand who are now helping Hmong refugees recover their independence.

The Hmong Expanded the Agenda of the Meeting

But the Hmong leaders had an agenda of their own. On top of the list was fear over proposals to cut off social services to the refugees after they had been in the country for 18 months; too short a time, they said, for an illiterate mountain man to learn English and vocational skills. Next on the list was deep concern over the constant bouncing back and forth around the country of thousands of Hmong looking for redoubt from unemployment, tough inner cities and isolation from other Hmong.

The federal government was concerned about the constant movement of Hmong also, but was more concerned about the concentration of Hmong in California, Wisconsin and Minnesota, a growing political problem because of the drain on state and county budgets.

If the goal of the meeting was to prepare the Hmong for an end to government support, the reality of the desperate situation facing the refugees derailed that plan. The leaders outlined a bleak future for the Hmong if they were not somehow stopped from moving constantly around the country, ever closer to the Central Valley and Wisconsin, where thousands of Hmong already lived, destitute and futureless.

The Highland Lao Initiative Is Launched

After the Washington meeting, the U.S. Office of Refugee Resettlement announced a plan to stabilize the Hmong population and keep more of them from moving to California. The government put $3 million into a campaign called the Highland Lao Initiative, aimed at bolstering social services in communities that were losing Hmong residents.

The program funneled money for 47 welfare and vocational programs for the Hmong in 44 cities outside of California. While 60 percent of the Hmong had been settled in or moved to California by the time the project began, 31,966 lived in cities in the Midwest, Northwest and Northeast.

During the time the project ran—from September 1983 to September 1984—the Hmong population in 15 of the targeted cities fell by only 436: from 15,302 to 14,866. The 36 families in Syracuse, NY, remained there and the populations of seven other cities in the program grew. Four Wisconsin cities included in the study grew a total of 1,054. Arrivals in Fresno, CA, the target of much Hmong migration, rose from approximately 10,000 to 13,000, but the rate of increase slowed.

While the results of the Highland Lao Initiative were not stunning, it outlined the framework for other projects that now hold the tenuous possibility of nudging the Hmong closer to the mainstream. The theory was, and still is, that the Hmong must be kept from concentrating in California, where unemployment is high and generous welfare benefits are a disincentive to work. To keep Hmong out of California, states and the federal government must provide educational and vocational opportunities for the refugees elsewhere.

"Really what the Highland Lao Initiative was, was a way to get services to the Hmong that were not available to them during the massive influx of refugees into the country after the war," says Toyo Biddle, of the U.S. Office of Refugee Resettlement.

"The Hmong were ignored when they arrived," agreed Wells Klein, director of the American Council for Nationalities Services, one of the largest private resettlement agencies in the country. "We didn't recognize they were so different from the Vietnamese, that they were illiterate and unskilled, so we had no special plans for them."

Small Work Projects Pay Off

Ten years after the Hmong began to arrive, things are beginning to change. With continued support from public assistance, Hmong are starting pilot projects, using what they know, to supplement their income and develop economic strategies for self-sufficiency. It is a gamble, but officials see it as a small but necessary step to fight unending welfare dependency. The projects are not the answer to the problems in the San Joaquin Valley, where too many Hmong, too little money, and too few jobs add up to a bleak future. But as one official said recently, "The person who finds a solution to the problems in the valley will be a certified genius."

In Wisconsin, Hmong in five communities are learning about the American economic system through cucumbers. What began as a local gardening project in Eau Claire, WI, has turned into a business for half a dozen Hmong communities throughout the state. In Eau Claire, Hmong refugee Yer Vang gathered $700 together from the Hmong community there and started a pickle cucumber farm. He arranged for technical assistance from the University of Wisconsin and for land from the county agricultural extension. The first year, 24 families working the land earned $23,000.

The idea spread and there are now Hmong pickle projects in Milwaukee, West Bend, Chippewa Falls, Eau Claire and two projects in Wausau. Each project has a buying agent and they contract their cucumber pickles to Gedney Pickle Co., of Minnesota.

"These projects are not really meant to get the Hmong off assistance," says Susan Levy, of the Wisconsin State Refugee Office, "But it supplements their income and teaches them important lessons about American economics."

The Planned Secondary Resettlement Project

Another offshoot of the Highland Lao Initiative was a project developed at the U.S. Office of Refugee Resettlement to draw Hmong away from California and Wisconsin with the promise of employment and the chance of bettering themselves. The project—called Planned Secondary Resettlement—pays for Hmong families to move from California and Wisconsin, and other highly impacted areas, to towns where Hmong are beginning to thrive.

Secondary resettlements are being planned in Dallas, Atlanta and the Blue Ridge Mountains of North Carolina, where small Hmong communities are experiencing nearly full employment and other benefits from living in areas where the cost of living is low and entry level jobs are available for non-English speakers.

"One reason why (the Dallas community thrives) is because of job opportunities there. Another factor is that at least half of the community was relatively skilled. They came to Dallas after they had received training in areas where they could not get a job," Biddle says.

"That community was pretty careful about saying to other people who might come to Dallas that it was a good place for

Hmong who want to work and want to work hard, but it was certainly not a place where there would be welfare available," she says.

Other thriving communities include the 36 to 40 families in Syracuse, NY, 1,800 people in Providence, RI, 129 people in Hartford, CT, and the 400 in Marion and Morgantown, NC.

In Providence, 90 percent of the Hmong are employed as machine operators, assembly workers, jewelry makers and sewing machine operators. There are also 80 students in college in Rhode Island, an historic step for the illiterate tribes of Laos.

Exemplary Communities Thrive

"These are exemplary communities. Its not really exemplary projects that are as important as exemplary places for the Hmong, where they can get jobs, buy houses and send their children to good schools," Biddle says.

"In places like the Valley or Wisconsin it is important to try all possible strategies . . . you can't leave any stone unturned, you have to attempt whatever is available, whatever methods might possibly work to help these people," she said.

In Dallas there is little talk of starting cooperative Hmong farms and self-help organizations, according to a study of Hmong resettlement done in 1983, because the Hmong there have jobs and houses.

But for those Hmong in California, Minnesota and Wisconsin who do not wish to pick up and move again, economic development programs are one of only a few alternatives to welfare dependency. Like novices in any economic endeavor, lessons for the Hmong can be expensive, especially when they pursue entrepreneurial projects rather than entering the job market for unskilled workers.

"The whole notion of an entrepreneurial person is rare with the Hmong. There are not many Hmong who are out there carrying on their own entrepreneurial project. Most of the economic development is group oriented. There is a lot more of that going on in the Highland Lao community than an individual entrepreneur striving to make himself rich," says Carol Leviton, of the Hmong/Highland Lao Development Fund.

The Hiawatha Valley Farm Project

In Minnesota, an ambitious farming project, fueled by dreams and good will, fell apart when promised financial backing never materialized. The Hiawatha Valley Farm Project taught the Hmong more about finances and legal problems than it did about American farming.

The project began as an ambitious dream to build a model farm where Hmong families could live, work and retain their cultural heritage. In late 1982, with money from a dozen Hmong families and a resettlement group called Church World Services, a purchase agreement was arranged with a farmer in Homer, MN, near the Wisconsin border. Nearly a dozen families moved to the farm, three hours drive from St. Paul, where they had lived.

In the summer of 1983, Ross Graves, who had helped organize the project, approached the state asking for funds to pay some of the Hmong and American workers. The state came up with the money, but learned later it had not been used to pay the salaries.

The State Attorney General and the Minnesota Department of Human Services began an investigation and the Hiawatha project began to unravel. The Hmong learned the land had not actually been paid for, as they believed. The owner of the farm filed a lawsuit against Church World Services and, in April 1984, the Hmong moved off the land and back to St. Paul.

"There were some very, very difficult months after they moved back," says Kretzmann. "They had almost no money and we were concerned about their diets, whether they had enough to eat."

But, the Hiawatha project had some positive fallout. Shoua Vang, who had organized the project, has gone on to use his expertise to organize agricultural economic development projects and has regrouped to form another Hmong farm cooperative in Hugo, MN, 15 minutes away from St. Paul, with funds of their own and support from Church World Services "which wanted to make amends" with the Hmong, according to Kretzmann. "Essentially, they have begun creating what they wanted to create, but the second time around."

New Hmong Refugees Arrive from Thailand

Toni Randolph

Since the end of the Vietnam War the United States has accepted more than 130,000 Hmong immigrants from war-torn Laos. A large percentage of these people have had a difficult time assimilating into the American culture. By 2000 between 30,000 and 40,000 Hmong refugees remained in Thailand, having lived for years in refugee camps because they believe they would be tortured or killed if they returned to Laos. In December 2003 the U.S. government agreed to a request from the Thai government to interview Hmong refugees for resettlement in the United States. Fifteen thousand of these refugees were accepted for resettlement into the United States. They began to arrive in the United States in 2004. In this selection Toni Randolph describes the reasons why this later wave of immigrants is likely to have an easier time assimilating than their predecessors.

Randolph is a journalist for Minnesota Public Radio.

Later this month [June 2004], Hmong refugees will begin arriving in Minnesota from Thailand. By the end of the year, the Twin Cities will have nearly 5,000 new Hmong residents. They'll join the more than 20,000 Hmong who began arriving here in the 1970s. While this new wave of refugees will have some obstacles to overcome when they arrive, they'll have some advantages their predecessors never did.

One of the biggest advantages that the newly arriving Hmong refugees will have is other Hmong here to welcome them. Cheu Lee, the publisher of the *Hmong Times*, says when his family came to the United States in 1976, it was a lonely arrival. "When we first arrived here in America, we had no

Hmong waiting at the airport. We had no relatives to greet you at the airport or at home—just yourself. And here, the newcomers [will] be greeted at the airport," he said.

Lee says friends and family will help the new arrivals learn their way around—literally and figuratively. For example, they won't have to figure out where to get staples of the Hmong diet such as rice and hot peppers like the first wave did. Hmong grocery stores have popped up all over the Twin Cities in the past 30 years.

Tzianeng Vang, 35, the chairman of Hmong Nationality Archives in Saint Paul, says he and his cousins are expecting about 20 family members to resettle in the Twin Cities by the end of the year. He says the new arrivals won't be coming out of a cultural vacuum. He says they've had exposure to urban life and American culture through relatives already living here. Vang says that wasn't the case when his family resettled in the U.S. in 1980, when he was about 10 years old.

"When we came we pretty much just came right out of the jungle, basically, and no exposure to technology nor urban lifestyle. So our mind frame or thinking cap was hunt and gather," he said.

First Wave of Immigrants Had Few Skills

Most of the first wave had few skills other than farming. Vang says some of these refugees have skills, such as jewelry-making, watch repair or sewing. And, Vang says, they have access to technology. In fact, some of them are keeping in touch with their relatives here by e-mail. Vang says his cousin e-mails him whenever he has questions about the resettlement. And Vang says when he traveled to the camp back in March he saw for himself how technology has changed the lives of many of the refugees in southeast Asia.

"Both in Thailand and Laos you can buy a cellphone off the street market and just start calling. You just use the calling card, you have a cellphone right there. Everybody that has a few dollars is able to own a cellphone," he said. But there are obstacles too. The "Wat," the Buddhist temple in Thailand north of Bangkok where these refugees have been living, is not an official refugee camp. As a result, the Hmong there have received few services from relief agencies, limited medical attention and little education. Few of the refugees speak English.

Tru Thao owns the Cedarhurst Mansion in Cottage Grove. He remembers how difficult it was for him when he resettled in the U.S. in 1975. "The hardest part for me was going to school and not speaking a word of English. I was put into the 5th grade. And I probably did not know what my teachers and peers were saying. I was very desperate to use the bathroom," he said.

Thao says he used to run two miles home after school every day to go to the bathroom because he didn't know the English words to tell his teacher.

Education Is the Key to Assimilation

About half of the 15,000 refugees living at the Wat are school-age children. About 2,500 new Hmong students could enroll in the Saint Paul public schools by the end of the year. School officials are already making plans to set up three transitional language centers in the elementary schools and expand them as necessary.

Thao says for refugees, education is one of the most important opportunities in the United States. "I think education has truly exposed us to our sense of capability and we continue to broaden our minds and souls. I think that has truly been a helpful factor for us, to continue to self-reflect and do the best we can," he said.

The first Hmong refugees are expected to arrive in as soon as two weeks. Local resettlement agencies are gearing up, as well as community and cultural organizations. Agencies are preparing to provide job-training and English-language classes for the Hmong refugees as they begin a new life in the United States. Ilene Her, 35, of the Council on Asian Pacific Minnesotans, says there's something bittersweet about their arrival compared to her own in 1976.

"For us anyway, it was like America was a new frontier, the whole community came. We were all equal. We all didn't know the language, we all had no money. And it wasn't established yet, the community wasn't established. And it was ours to establish in that sense that we were all working together, we were all building something," she said.

The new wave won't have that sense of adventure. But Her says they won't feel the sadness of the first wave because the foundation is already in place. "The first wave, they, just the sense of depression, they were so sad. They were in a country that was so new. They didn't know anything about how to interact in this society. And this next wave won't feel that sadness, won't feel that depression. They will be welcomed, they will be loved and we will help them as much as we can," she said.

Now this new wave can begin to make its own mark on Minnesota.

CHAPTER 3

COMING *TO*
AMERICA

Hmong Youth Settle into American Culture

Hmong Women's Lives Change in America

Nancy D. Donnelly

Substantial differences exist between traditional Hmong view-points of gender roles and the viewpoints more prevalent in America. In Hmong society the marriage and wedding traditions alone are governed by eighteen unwritten laws, many of which are unheard of in Western society. Traditionally, men are at the top of the social ladder, and women, in every age group, are con-sidered less than men. Men control the money and make the de-cisions for the entire family. In this selection Nancy D. Donnelly presents a picture of Hmong women as they begin to move away from these traditions and adopt the traditions of the Americans around them. The author does this by explaining the traditions they are leaving behind and the support for equality that the American culture gives them. Hmong women are making more money, which elevates their power in the family past traditional bounds. The author discusses what it may mean to Hmong cul-ture in America to have the traditional familial bonds broken, as women begin to embrace American institutions such as marry-ing for love and participating in divorce.

Donnelly is a cultural anthropologist who spent years work-ing with Hmong refugees in Seattle, Washington.

The key to understanding gender attitudes among first-generation Hmong refugees lies in their universal insis-tence that they will remain Hmong as long as they can main-tain a certain set of social relationships within the household—an insistence on continuity, on nonchanging so-cial structure. The particular social forms can be identified not by the actual content or goals of actions, but by the lines

Nancy D. Donnelly, *Changing Lives of Refugee Hmong Women.* Seattle: University of Washington Press, 1997. Copyright © 1994 by the University of Washington Press. All rights reserved. Reproduced by permission.

of respect and authority that they embody. These place each person in two hierarchies: gender and age. Old men are given more respect than young men, who receive more than boys. Old women are honored and their wishes catered to by their families, but while old men and women are more nearly equal than young men and women, the amount of respect accorded old women is still less than that accorded old men. Females in each age category are placed beneath male contemporaries, because they are female, and women always owe respect to men.

Hmong, like other refugees resettled to a new location, reconstruct as best they can their already understood social worlds, and overcome imperfections in the reconstruction by substitution and overlooking difference. In general, incoming Hmong refugees do not seek new lives, they seek the same lives in a new location, and where possible they use their new opportunities to bolster preexisting social conceptions. This is clearly illustrated by their needlework sales. The beautiful batik, appliqué work, and embroidery made by Hmong women were not marketplace items in Laos, but were intended for household use and ritual exchanges signifying social and emotional attachments. In the profoundly different environment of Seattle, however, traditional sources of family subsistence and of wealth (farming, opium trade) were in short supply. Hmong men could not easily turn to economic use in America the military and political skills they had developed during wartime. Meanwhile Hmong women, encouraged by American admiration for their needlework, and having available to them the cultural model of the effective and clever Hmong wife, turned their sewing skill to money by selling adapted pieces in a market economy mediated mainly by American volunteer advisors.

Making Money Shifts the Power

This activity illustrates a recombination and reconstruction of bits of strategic activity already available in Hmong culture, turning them to fit a new set of needs and opportunities. In the process, needlework intended for the market changed stylistically, alienated as it was from social and ritual use in Hmong households. Family and ritual exchanges continued, with new objects as well as old carrying the burden of social attachments; for instance, sisters-in-law made up coordinated outfits by exchanging store-bought clothes (a new set of objects), even as gifts of baby carriers to new mothers continued, unaffected by the marketing of baby carriers. Meanwhile, the profits of needlework sales entered the family economy, where their use was determined by traditional ideas of authority within households. Underlying cultural meanings were not damaged or reshaped by this shuffling of the objects used in symbolic behavior or subsistence support. The definition of Hmong women as creators of beauty, skilled in devotion to their families, and embedded in a social order dominated by men, remained intact.

The politicized nature of two needlework cooperatives can be included in this pattern of taking the materials at hand and restructuring them to conform to existing cultural models. Here the materials were the cooperatives and the model was hierarchical control. Using familiar strategies, accepted (even when disliked) by other Hmong, local Hmong leaders experienced in the former power structure in Laos strove persistently to coopt the cooperatives to a vision of Hmong social structure directly derived from their old-country experiences. Their complex statements of motivation and their persistence even in spite of unprofitability, lift their actions beyond simple self-interest. They acted as they knew how, because they knew how, and did not change methods although they recognized their inadequacy, because they did not know how to change. The problematic results of their endeavors demonstrate that control over people depends on the quality of the available rewards and threats. This is evidence, not of newly developing meanings to explain changed behavior in a new setting, but of old explanations transplanted.

Hmong Marriages

Underlying gender constructs seemed not to have been threatened by Hmong women's textile marketing. But another arena of cultural action appeared promising in the search for possible shifts in the symbols that support behavior. Overt differences in the rituals and events comprising Hmong marriages were immediately apparent, but whether these indicated underlying change was not. Kia Her and Tsu Ly's marriage was arranged using conveniences like the telephone and money orders. The groom's family bridged distance with cars and airplane, and offered Christian prayers rather than spirit offerings. These innovations, however, were entirely subordinate to the older meaning attached to the process of marriage—that the bride was now under the protection and control of her husband's family, and her children would be legitimate members of his clan. . . .

In the wedding negotiation . . . many small differences arose in procedure because of the new milieu, some appearing to hinder and some to facilitate the preservation of traditional form. Prognostications could not be made from the toes of the gift chickens because supermarket chickens have no toes. The negotiators preferred nonalcoholic Sprite over vodka, so a source of cleverness and fun in setting terms of the marriage (befuddling the other negotiator to benefit your own side) was not available. A dispute arose over the value of butchered pork compared with a pig on the hoof, the standard of value in Laos. Because time was short and one side lacked a seasoned negotiator, songs were abbreviated and a clause excusing errors had to be added to the contract. Bride wealth was paid in cash, not the silver of tradition. While these aspects of the negotiation do not seem to accord with tradition, other new elements appeared more congruous. Faraway but significant relatives had come by air, one from Santa Ana, one from France. The contract could be typed, meaning its terms were more securely set down than the verbal contracts usual in

Laos. The negotiation could be videotaped for distant relatives. Many such differences could be cited, but ultimately the meaning of the negotiation itself remained constant. The bride was honorably shifted to the care of her new husband's family, with the offer of bride wealth demonstrating the approval of the husband's elder relatives, and its acceptance signaling the approval of the bride's. The contract reinforced continuing relationships between and within the two families. The elder men of both families indicated their status in regard to the young couple, since only they could make the contract. The young people accepted the propositions that without this contract they would not be married (no other could suffice), and that with this contract no other was necessary (this one was sufficient). Despite its flaws and abbreviation, this negotiation provided an acceptable framework for reproducing and validating Hmong kinship ties.

Breaking a Marriage Contract

The same appears to have been true even of the troubled negotiations over the wedding of Mee and Song. . . . Nearly all the actual circumstances of life, the topics covered in the contract, the later subjects of dispute, Mee's method of escape from her unsatisfactory situation, and the financial difficulties differed from those of life in Laos. Yet even in this conflict, vital elements of Hmong social structure were reproduced. The young couple placed themselves under the vigorous control of the older generation. Song's elder, a traditionalist, took a romantic attitude—if the children loved each other, their marriage could not fail. But Mee's father, who was working diligently toward economic security, felt quite differently. To him, poverty was hateful. His emphasis on economic progress and his despair over his daughter's poor future looks Americanized until we remember how well his new son-in-law fit the Hmong cultural model of the poor orphan who marries up, and how well he himself fit the model of the infuriated father-in-law impotent to prevent it. There are Hmong cultural models for these behaviors. The girl's model in this case is the King of Heaven's daughter, solving all the orphan's problems with her magical powers. This was where romanticism ended, when the disillusioned girl, instead of striving by her labor and generosity to improve her husband's lot, decamped. Hers was a dissonant act, which had to be reinterpreted in Hmong terms to become the result of female meddling, before the elder men could take the initiative again and a formulaic face-saving compromise could eventually be reached. Since the acts of girls "do not matter," Mee's disturbing flight could be smoothed over. As with Kia Ly's defection, the individual act of rebellion posed more hazard to Mee's place in Hmong society than to Hmong society. Such incidents were part of life in Laos, with no structural change required to accommodate them.

What happens when motivations seem to run contrary to the ideals of Hmong social life?. . . Mai use[d] the American legal system to free herself from her husband and go back to her natal family. In Laos this would have been an impossible goal, given the feebleness of her complaints compared with traditional grounds for divorce, the primacy of the social rule that women upon marriage join their husband's clan, and men's preference not to offend other clans. Hmong strategies to resolve domestic conflict failed, as neither husband nor wife would take advice, and an anomalous strategy succeeded, as Mai's male relatives covertly helped her utilize American legal processes and Americans who could guide her through the courts. Mai expressed the unusual wish to be more like her brother, literate and self-reliant, and she wanted her children but not her husband. Although strongly criticized by proper Hmong women, she retained the support of her male relatives. Her use of outside resources was incorporated within an acceptable Hmong strategy for unhappy wives, seeking the protection of her own clan. This would not have sufficed if her male supporters had wanted social ties with her husband, but he was both weak and disliked. They overlooked the conventional strategy that required urging her to return, since Mai emphasized her propriety in other ways, giving up her desire for education, spending her time in childcare, sewing and cooking, and placing herself under her brother's control. If Mai had not had relatives willing to help her, if she had pursued her nonwomanly desire for personal strength, or if she had relied more heavily on her American friends, she might have been forced out of Hmong society. In this configuration of mixed strategies, however, the overriding image was of a troubled Hmong woman seeking the help of her natal family.

Improper Women

In looking for the manner in which lives change, it is important to look not only at changing goals, but also at how such goals are achieved.... Particular goals are themselves in part determined by what possible strategies can be used to achieve them. This is apparent in Mai's efforts to escape the threat of domestic violence and her husband's expressed contempt for her. She focused her efforts on divorce, while in Laos she might well have had to be satisfied with oral assurances of physical safety. Her ultimate goal—freedom from fear—remained the same, and she achieved it in the United States by using the same strategic style she would have used in Laos, putting herself under the protection of her male relatives. The actual lines of action she and they constructed, however, included new elements in the form of non-Hmong assistance and the American court system. Only because these elements could be subordinated to an overriding Hmong strategy could they be acceptable action for a Hmong woman. For the same reason, the range of acceptable actions for Hmong women has expanded to include divorce. Although divorce is still confined, in the eyes of "proper" women, to "improper" women, divorced women can nonetheless be improper *Hmong* women.

The reason divorce is improper behavior seems to be related to women crossing over the age and gender line that assigns contracts to the sphere of elder males. If a woman meddles with divorce to benefit her own life, this is improper behavior because she was not one of the people making the marriage contract. In the traditional view, the contract linked two families of men. Family ties are strongest between related men, and women think of themselves as the glue that holds these families together. The long-range implication of divorce initiated by the wife is that the marriage contract is between husband and wife. This is the American view, assumed by American courts, but it opens a Pandora's box for Hmong social structure. Where the society itself consists of links between families, the definition of family is crucial.

Lives Change over Time

Other hints of change in the definition of family are visible in the very proper [Hmong] wedding party. . . . [As at a wedding party in] Chiengmingmai, Thailand . . . the older men and women [ate] separately, but, [at a wedding party in Seattle] especially among the younger people, changes in the symbolism of marriage seemed evident. Women had a more central role, having arranged the party, and the bride stood at the door with her mother-in-law greeting guests. In Chiengmingmai, the party and its exchanges were arranged by men, who greeted the guests, while the bride stayed reticently well behind her husband and deep within the house. In Seattle, English was the language used to celebrate the formation of the couple, who danced publicly together to romantic Laoized rock tunes, whispering romantic phrases. The effect of such modernized behavior is to emphasize the presence of a couple, the basis of a nuclear family, rather than (as in Chiengmingmai) the creation of a daughter-in-law with her potential for continuing her husband's descent line.

Over time, the Hmong families I knew in America were coming to seem more like nuclear families based on married couples and less like extended families based on ties between brothers. I attribute some subtle changes to the effect of the larger American society, which had clear assumptions regarding individuals and did not assume family solidarity at any cost. Wives, even children, are expected to have opinions and individual goals in American society. Teachers, doctors, social workers, co-workers, and employers all expect individual family members to speak up, decide for themselves, and look out for their own benefit. Christianity, especially the fundamentalist Protestantism espoused by many Hmong in America, assumes individual salvation and responsibility, and the equal value of all souls. American legal process assumes that women are equal to men before the law, and in problematic cases deals with catch-hand marriage in terms of kidnap or rape.

Keeping a Tally

The aspects of life in which traditional Hmong can most easily resist change are those where a tally can be kept. This is clearly visible in terms of money exchanges and control of money within the household; it is easy to see who brought home how much, who made spending decisions, and where the money went. In these areas—income, household expense, bride wealth, financial contributions to relatives' projects, expenses for future planning, travel, education—power over decisions, which was in male hands in Laos, could be guarded by men, because there was a convenient and precise measure through which the amount of control could be determined.

But other areas of life were less amenable to close accounting. What did it portend if Hmong women promoted Christianity, especially when they said it was because Christianity rejected polygyny and taught the equality of all souls? How visible was that to the men who might be jealous of their privileges? Would the men object if they recognized these reasons among other, more spiritual ones? What if women no longer sewed clothes for men, but strictly their own festival wear and commercial exchange items? If a mother signed the child's school permission slips instead of a father? If the mother, not the father, conversed with a child's doctor? If children of both sexes were outside parental control most days? If a woman successfully ignored an oral contract? If women as well as men learned the requirements of citizenship and the language of the dominant society? If a girl cried foul when a youth forced her into an unwanted marriage, and successfully avoided marriage? If wedding gifts were given directly to the young couple instead of being channeled through the bride's father? If bride wealth was sometimes not paid? If the durability of a marriage could not be foretold from the toe curl of toeless supermarket chickens? If a few Hmong girls began to marry non-Hmong, while the few divorced women forced from Hmong society did not perish? If the King County Superior Court assigned child custody on the basis of parent's closeness to the child rather than parent's social power?

All these instances are alterations in the expression of social power and the capacity to express it. Most of them are hard to calculate in terms of actual advantage—which is the point. Because they cannot be measured, they became ambiguous, ungraspable. Often they seem trivial or are even invisible to the people involved. Still, whether large or small, unavoidable or discretionary, they taught their participants something about the possibilities for action in a new environment. As these and a thousand other incidents multiply in the lives of resettled Hmong, their weight tends to lean toward more egalitarian interactions between men and women. The more nearly equal conceptualization of men and women current in the United States has entered Hmong households via such changes. Some Hmong ideas of gender are being reexpressed, and the idea of family itself has changed in ways that echo the new environment. American cultural concepts about romance, the expectation that both men and women will work and make decisions, the individuality stressed in public schools, and new ideas about how to conduct a wedding can be pointed out as influences from the new society, especially on younger Hmong.

The Seeds of Gender Equality

If this viewpoint is true, Hmong might be expected to adopt new tenets of egalitarianism as part of Hmong identity and reexplain Hmong social relations in terms of gender equality. The seeds of gender equality are present in Hmong folk tales and in the concept that both men and women need each other to achieve maturity, even if they are not always expressed in Hmong social practice. From these seeds, novel lines of action might arise to fit new experiences, without Hmong having to invent wholly new and idiosyncratic personal interpretations of events, without the need to justify new behavior by stepping outside their native culture, without resorting to alien ideas. Since submissiveness was usually called for in the lives of Hmong women in Laos, this capacity was woven into the social behavior of Hmong women generally; but when assertiveness was demanded, a different, yet still appropriate, cultural model—the vigorous Hmong wife promoting her family's benefit—was available and could be taken up. The two styles of action contradict each other, but both are available within the range of models available to Hmong women.

Cultures abound in such an overrichness of possibilities, of inconsistencies and contradictions in cultural models. This provides the resiliency that may let the culture itself survive even traumatic shifts of circumstance. The way action is organized survives even as its goals or ends change to accommodate different surroundings, different needs. But perhaps it is not appropriate to be too optimistic about Hmong culture. The contested ground of control over women's lives engenders terrific bitterness and pain for first generation resettled refugees, as assumptions shift about propriety and possibility for women and men. Perhaps this can be called cultural lag. . . .

Even when the values or goals of a community shift or surface behaviors change through interactions with a new environment, the basic organization of a society need not necessarily be changing. Change in this deeper sense must include alterations in cultural capacities or the symbols that give them meaning. These are what produce all the different strategies of action that are manifested in behavior. Overt actions illustrate the contact points between cultural capacities and the exterior world.

This study, based on work with mostly middle-aged refugees resettled less than eight years, found less culture change than expected. It would be very helpful to study the lives of adolescents, especially Hmong who came to the United States as quite young children, to record how they are faring in their mixed milieu. Future research on the attitudes of the next generation, particularly if undertaken by the very Hmong now growing to maturity in the American educational system, will provide a fascinating comparison for this and other studies now appearing on the Hmong.

Gender attitudes are only one area of the research into social change that could be undertaken among resettled Hmong. . . . In particular, inquiry into Hmong Christian religious ideas would be very useful in trying to understand changing Hmong ideas regarding gender, but Christianity is an area I have hardly touched. Every aspect of life partakes of the experiences and demands of every other aspect. Hmong can change their economic and educational goals, their clothing styles and household paraphernalia, parts of their vocabulary (in some households, the language itself) and still be certain they are Hmong. In the chameleon world of surface change, goals shift and strategies of action gradually accommodate to tasks rephrased in a new environment. Dissonant symbolic messages picked up from outside Hmong culture jostle against ideas taught at home, and must be reconciled. Religion may provide a major mechanism of resolution in helping people struggling with change to reorder their ideas in new symbolic shapes, integrating their new lives with the old. Christian influence is a complex issue in these resolutions that needs future exploration.

The Problem of Hmong Gangs

Brendan McGarvey

*As the Hmong youth become more and more Americanized,
some have rejected their parents' culture and some have even begun to join heavily armed street gangs. As Brendan McGarvey
describes in this selection, not as many Hmong youth are interested in gang activity as other Asian groups. Law enforcement is
concerned about the increase in Hmong gang activity. McGarvey
writes that some gang members are being recruited by notorious
gangs such as the United Bamboo Triad, the Bloods, and the
Crips. These gangs are involved in prostitution, the drug trade,
and illegal gambling. Police are concerned that Asian and African American gangs will collaborate and increase the level of
crime in the United States.*

McGarvey is a reporter for the Philadelphia City Paper.

There is a house in Bryn Mawr [Pennsylvania] with a hid-
den room. Inside this room are stored the spoils of
America's secret wars: Chinese swords, ivory carvings from
Thailand, religious relics from Tibet and Laos, American
M-16s from the war in Vietnam and Kalashnikov AK-47s car-
ried by the armies of drug warlords in what used to be called
Burma.

This Bryn Mawr home belongs to an Irish-American who
worked as a helicopter pilot for a CIA front company called
Air America. Air America flew clandestine missions in Southeast Asia in the '60s and '70s. A neighborhood kid in South-
west Philly, this man joined the Army, learned to fly helicopters, and then went to work for Air America and other CIA
front companies in the late 1950s.

The pilot says he helped secretly evacuate the Dalai Lama when Chinese troops in Tibet began targeting spiritual leaders there. The pilot also says he flew missions to North Vietnam and Laos, sometimes rescuing downed American pilots or special forces teams caught behind enemy lines in the 1960s and '70s. He heroically risked his life many times to save both soldiers and civilians.

But as much as his colleagues were impressed with the bravery of this Air America pilot, the chopper pilot himself felt that, compared with the Hmong tribesmen he encountered on his many missions, his own courage in no way resembled the fierce warrior ethos of the Hmong guerrillas.

The Hmong Were Isolated When They First Arrived in America

The Hmong, an ethnic Chinese people who populate the mountainous regions of Laos, Vietnam, Burma and Thailand, were used as scouts, snipers and secret warriors by American Green Berets and other U.S. military special forces units because they were extremely brave under fire and skillful at guerrilla warfare.

But when American involvement ended in Vietnam in 1975, the Hmong were left to their own fate. Those who escaped with their families spent years in Asian refugee camps before finally being resettled in the United States.

West Philadelphia is one of the places the Hmong refugees eventually came to call home. For many Hmong families here in Philadelphia, the culture shock was overwhelming. Men renowned for their fierceness in battle in their own land felt like defeated, isolated and economically impoverished victims in this new place.

Because of this isolation from mainstream society, Asian gangs often targeted the Hmong for extortion and shakedown schemes. But the new generation of Hmong, some born in

America and some born in Asian refugee camps, are acting quite differently from their parents.

Many of the younger generation of Hmong are choosing to reject their parents' culture and are embracing all things American. A significant number of West Philadelphia Hmong teenagers have adopted the hip-hop music and street slang of their predominantly African-American neighborhood.

And a small percentage of Hmong have now formed their own criminal gangs. Tired of seeing their parents' small businesses victimized by Asian thugs, primarily Vietnamese-American street gangs like the VTK, and feeling victimized themselves at school and at home by thugs—the Hmong gangs have begun to carry weapons.

Gang Involvement Has Increased

In the last year, according to police sources, there has been a significant increase in Hmong gang activity. Still, it is not anywhere on the scale of crime committed by other Asian organized-crime groups in the Delaware Valley. But what worries police is what may happen in the future.

In other parts of the country, Asian crime experts are seeing a disturbing phenomenon: Hmong gang members, along with Vietnamese-American gangsters, are being recruited into the Crips and Bloods gangs. The Crips and the Bloods are two of the largest street gangs in the U.S. Both started on the streets of Los Angeles and are primarily composed of African-Americans, with a very small Latino and white membership.

But law enforcement agents have found evidence of Hmongs joining Bloods and Crips gangs on the West Coast and in the Minneapolis-St. Paul area and central Wisconsin. And police have discovered a link between young Hmong gang members in Philadelphia and Minneapolis—a gang associate in Philly with family ties in Minneapolis.

"In Philly," one police source told *City Paper*, "you could eventually see Asian and black gangs selling Southeast Asian heroin and cooperating on everything from illegal gambling rackets to prostitution rings." The Philadelphia police source calls it the Asian-black-Asian connection.

"You have drug warlords in the Golden Triangle, who with the help of the United Bamboo triad, now have the ability to move heroin and other drugs from Asia to the West Coast without the middlemen. The drug lords can now sell directly to the Bloods and Crips in L.A. Eventually, some young Hmong gang member in West Philly is going to end up being the source for half the heroin in our region. That's a scary thought. And a very good possibility."

Breaking Away from Tradition

Christopher Loke

Many Hmong youth in the United States face the challenge of living in two cultures at one time. At home they are brought up with Hmong traditions, but at school and outside the home they are immersed in the American culture. Many, like Na Vongsa Vue, find the traditional demands presented by their elders too restrictive. They break away from the traditional and ultimately alienate their family in the process. In this selection Christopher Loke interviews Na Vongsa about his break with tradition and family. Na Vongsa recounts the events leading up to his banishment from his family for not wanting to marry the stranger they chose for him. Despite the difficulties so far, however, Na Vongsa states that he is proud to be Hmong and will honor his people by choosing his own destiny.

At the time this article was published, Loke was a student of journalism at Utah State University.

Na Vongsa Vue was only 21 when he was asked to marry. But Vue had other plans. He wanted to marry a woman he loved instead of a stranger.

Even so, he could not deny the fact that he was betrothed. He was forced. And things got nasty when he wanted a way out.

The night was quite windy outside a double-story house at Hickory, N.C., on a summer evening. The atmosphere was calm. But inside the house, tension rose. Vue's mother was hitting her chest with her hand. She was screaming, yelling and crying.

"You listen to me!" she said. "I raise you and I will determine who you marry! You are my son, and we are not like the whites! Do not forget where you come from and your heritage! You listen to me!"

Christopher Loke, "Life in Two Cultures a Maze for a Hmong Named 'Crazy Rat on Opium,'" http://www.hardnewscafe.usu.edu, June 16, 2003. Reproduced by permission.

All the while, Vue had his hands over his ears, his eyes squinting closed, trying to look away.

"You look at me when I am talking to you!" his mother said, stomping the kitchen counter with her fist. The yelling and scolding had been going on for the past few days soon after Vue expressed his desire to not marry a stranger. He wanted to call off the betrothal. It all started off with naggings here and there. But today, all hell broke lose. His mother was crying, beating her chest, kicking the walls, and wailing with horrific agony. If her son disobeyed her, he would have been better off dead. He would be disowned.

Leaving the Family

And Vue was well aware of the consequences of his decision. He was aware of his culture.

"If you don't stop, you'll wake up one day and I'll not be here anymore. I will leave and not come back!" Vue said. A week later, Vue had his luggage ready at the door. He was going away.

"What is all this?" his mother asked, pointing to the bags piled up at the door.

"I am leaving, Ma," Vue said. And that was the day he flew to Utah.

Such is the way of the Hmong people. You either live up to your parents' expectations or you are banished, Vue says.

Although raised in the United States, Vue has always known that he is different from the people around him. He is Asian, 5-foot-6, has spiky hair, and likes sports cars. But those are not the things that single him out from the rest of the American population. Although he looks like any Asian-Americans in his community, goes to school and works like everyone else, there is one aspect of his life that is unique. He is Hmong, a tribal people who come from the mountains in the jungles of Laos.

Hmong people are extremely traditional and superstitious, Vue says. They are expected to be committed to their own people and traditions no matter how absurd they may be. And in this modern world, the call to carry on the old traditions is stronger, he says.

"Often times, being too traditional can be bad," he says. "For example, you could be discriminated upon."

Living with Discrimination

To Vue, when he moved to North Carolina, he was shocked to find discrimination and prejudices everywhere against his people. He was never treated the same, he says.

"One reason I came to Utah was because my friend, Travis, lived here, and also because this is Utah, the place where friendly Mormons live," he says. "But unfortunately, there is more discrimination here compared to North Carolina."

Shaking his head, Vue inhales a deep breath and releases a sigh.

"We did not choose to be here," he says, his tone a notch higher, firmer. "Americans brought us here because my people had no choice. We helped the Americans fight the Vietnam War because they asked us to. And as a result, we got kicked out of our country."

Vue now stands, pacing back and forth in his room.

"We came because we had no choice, and they didn't treat us right," he says. "Why are they prejudiced? Why are they like that?"

The room is quiet. There is no response. No answer. He sits back on the chair and props his head on one hand and starts to think. Another deep breath.

"If only they know the truth," he says, rather gravely.

To Vue, living in the U.S. as a Hmong has been difficult. First, he has to uphold his family virtues and traditions. Second, he claims to be discriminated upon. He says his family, for some reason, has been treated differently by the Americans.

Hearing Stories of the War

Vue recalls the stories his father would tell him about the war.

"My father fought for the Americans in the war, you know," he says, chest up, head up high. "And still, they didn't help him back."

Vue says his father would work very hard to survive when he was growing up in California. His family basically lived in a "ghetto," he says.

"I remember one day when my father came running into the house, cheering," Vue says. "'I made seven bucks per hour now because I just got a raise,' he said. I was like, 'That's not much. I start out with seven bucks just working here.'"

Vue says whenever he sees his father, he automatically assumes a sense of responsibility. He needs to uphold his heritage and his culture. But sometimes it is difficult, especially when two cultures collide.

Raised in the U.S. as an LDS [Latter Day Saint for Mormon], he is often faced with cultural conflicts. The whole betrothal incident is an example, he says. After his family joined the LDS faith when he was 8, he says things felt weird. Because the strong Hmong traditions that his family practiced sometimes clashed with LDS church values, he often questioned his father.

"One day, I asked my father, 'Are we members or partial members of the church?'" he says. "And my father said we were half and half."

For example, Vue points out that he is supposed to marry his own kind, while the LDS church encourages its members to marry within the same faith. In other words, he says, he will have to marry a Hmong Mormon in order to satisfy both ends.

But to Xou Yang, another Hmong here in the valley, things are a little different. First, he is not LDS, thus the pressure to find a Hmong Mormon is not there. Second, Yang was born in the U.S. He was not raised in a strong traditional setting.

"One thing I like about being Hmong is that we help each other. Your business is my business," he says. "For example, my uncle wanted to buy a mall and everyone in the family chipped in and helped raise $1 million."

But being Hmong is not always good news, Yang says. He says the one thing he does not like about Hmong people is that they are always related to gangster fights and the macho image.

Vue, on the other hand, thinks that being Hmong is something to be proud of despite the prejudice upon his people.

"I like the fact that my dad was in the war," he says. "He would tell me all the stories when he fought in the war. I wish I have stories like that to tell my kids."

The Traditions of Food Remain

But when it comes to food, Vue admits that Hmong cuisine is very different and—many times—weird to Americans.

"We eat intestines and organs of animals," he says. "If you're Hmong, you're taught not to waste. When you live up in the mountains where food is scarce, you learn to eat everything. When you kill a cow, you do not waste a single thing."

Vue stretches his hands and smacks his lips.

"You know, I wouldn't want to be anyone else in the world," he says, smiling, sitting straight up. "At least I can say that I am pure Hmong. If I am dog, I would be worth thousands of dollars."

He laughs, mouth gaps open, tapping the table with his fingers at intervals. "You want to know the meaning of my name?" he asks.

He explains that Na means rodent, while Vongsa means opium. Vue, he says, is just a last name, but if it is said incorrectly, it could mean crazy. The Hmong language is a language based on tones, he says. A slightest shift of tone could change the meaning of a word completely, he says.

"So, in other words, I am a crazy rat on opium!"

Vue now ventures into the kitchen and starts to prepare some traditional spring rolls dipped in fish sauce. In a few moments, the kitchen will be filled with the aroma of Hmong food. Before long, his apartment will be the hibernating place of the smoky smell of dead pungent fish and salted pork meat. Garlic and chili will add to the sting of the nose-watering odor. To Vue's white roommates, it will be as if tear gas has been released.

But to Vue, it will be the pure enjoyment of Hmong food—his soul food.

Hmong Children Turn to the Courts for Help

Brian Bonner

Before coming to America, Hmong family and neighbor disputes were handled by a coalition of clan leaders, who were all men. Now in America, many of the first-generation Hmong still want to handle their differences in this old way, staying clear of the American justice system. However, the new generation of Hmong is breaking with tradition and turning to the police and the court system to help them resolve family matters. In this selection Brian Bonner describes a trial involving two Hmong sisters who sought help from authorities and accused their father of sexually abusing them. While some in the Hmong community were outraged, others thought the trial a step in the right direction, writes Bonner.

Bonner is a journalist for the St. Paul Pioneer Press *in St. Paul, Minnesota.*

The live chicken in the St. Paul courtroom was the most obvious sign that *State of Minnesota vs. Za Xiong* wasn't a run-of-the-mill case.

The Hmong defendant wanted to sacrifice the chicken and drink its blood to prove he was telling the truth when he denied sexually abusing his teen-age daughters. Xiong, who practices shamanism, told his lawyer that the spirits would kill whoever drank the blood and lied. He also wanted prosecutors and his daughters to partake.

Xiong never got to try his method of justice. Ramsey County District Judge Charles Flynn left it to the jury to decide the truth. The panel ... convicted Xiong on one charge of fondling his younger daughter, while it acquitted him of two other charges.

Xiong's case was ... [an] example of the greater willingness of Hmong children to take their problems outside the family in search of justice. Left to traditional Hmong culture, male clan leaders would have investigated the girls' allegations and resolved the dispute internally.

"It is a very rare case," said Chang Vang, a youth counselor with Lao Family Community of Minnesota Inc., of the incest charges. "It could be the beginning of them coming out."

To some, especially those who think the girls told the truth, the case also revealed the ostracism that Hmong children face when they buck tradition.

Some Think Youth Manipulate the System

To others, especially those who think the girls lied, the case shows how Hmong children manipulate the U.S. system for their own devious ends.

In this case, more than two dozen relatives and friends filled Flynn's courtroom. They contributed $10,000 to hire a private defense attorney, Robert Miller. Many others signed petitions proclaiming their belief in Xiong's innocence.

By contrast, the girls were accused—by their father and other relatives—of lying to escape discipline and chores at home. The girls had little, if any, visible support among the courtroom spectators. They are currently in foster care as their father awaits a possible four-year prison sentence.

"I think it's quite sad that nobody is willing to think that maybe he did something," said Ramsey County prosecutor Elizabeth Beltaos. "The first person they told is their mom, and she didn't do anything."

A Wisconsin prosecutor said he witnessed a similar backlash against a Hmong girl in a pending incest case against her father.

"There remains a real risk of ostracism," said Scott Horne, district attorney in La Crosse, Wis., a city with several thousand Hmong. "The Hmong community did become involved. The girl was branded a liar. There's been progress in terms of reuniting her with the Hmong community, but it's been a painful process," Horne said.

Despite the risk of being shunned, Horne said, "we have seen kids coming forward with information about things committed in the family, whether it's physical abuse, sexual abuse or domestic violence." He expects more Hmong children will be willing to bypass traditional constraints as their contact with non-Hmong children expands.

"The fact of abuse is probably not accepted well in the Hmong culture," said Horne. "Maybe the allegations haven't been brought forward in the past, and the acceptance of the reality of sexual abuse isn't there. I think there is denial."

Family Abuse Charges Are Shocking

Supporters of Xiong said they were shocked by the charges and guilty verdict because incest is virtually unheard of in Hmong communities—whether in the United States, China, or Laos. (About 150,000 Hmong live in the United States; most are refugees from the Vietnam War.) The idea of incest is so taboo that marriages within a clan are forbidden.

But Kai Xiong—a relative of the defendant—said Hmong clan leaders listened fairly to both sides. They concluded, he said, that the girls lacked credibility. Kai Xiong said one of the girls told him she would do anything to get out of the home.

The father, in an interview, said the girls were lying to escape cooking, cleaning and caring for 11 younger siblings. He also said his girls had been skipping school, hanging around "troublemakers" and staying out late without permission.

Xiong said he didn't blame his daughters for the charges brought against him. Instead, he blamed prosecutors, police officers, social workers and a Lutheran pastor—the first out-sider in whom the girls first confided—with "coaching" his daughters' testimony.

While prosecutors saw Xiong as using a classic blame-the-victim strategy, a Hmong counselor said there had been instances in which Hmong children made up stories to escape the household.

Juries Are Sympathetic to Hmong Children

"In many cases, the children want to move out of the home where they can live freely and nobody would ask them to do anything," said Wang Xang Xiong, the parent-teen coordinator for the Hmong American Partnership.

The jury in Xiong's case, however, concluded . . . that his younger daughter told the truth when she alleged that her father had engaged in sexual contact with her. But the jury acquitted him of the most serious charge—that he sexually penetrated the daughter: It also acquitted him of another charge of sexual contact with an older daughter. A juror, speaking on condition of anonymity, said the older daughter was less credible. She was seen as "just supporting the younger sister," this juror said.

The panelist said Xiong's defense—and the courtroom support that he garnered—revealed more about the highly patriarchal nature of Hmong society than anything else. "They seem to have a very father-centered culture," said the juror. "That's what I got out of it: He's a leader in the community and in the family, and who is going to (stand) up against him?"

Caitlin Mai Lee, a Hmong college student who has written about feminist issues, agreed with the juror. Lee believes that abuse in Hmong homes often goes unreported because Hmong females, especially, fear they will become outcasts if they seek justice through the American system.

In general, Lee said, "we're not at the point where we can actually take somebody to court. I don't think we will be there for a long time. I, myself, would not take somebody to court."

She also said many younger Hmong females doubt they will get a fair hearing inside the traditional clan system. "If you are going up against somebody who is older than you, especially if that someone is male, they will come out on top," Lee said.

Young Hmong Musicians

Nzong Xiong

Many immigrant populations have brought their musical tradi-tions to America and added the richness of new sounds to the country's musical landscape. Many Hmong youth are also creat-ing music that combines the tradition of the Hmong music and the influence of American styles including R&B and rock. In this selection Nzong Xiong describes the new young Hmong Ameri-can bands that are becoming increasingly popular. Bolstered by the crossover of Latin music into the mainstream in recent years, these new Hmong bands are hoping to get a big break and be-come a hit in America.

Xiong is a contributing journalist for such newspapers as the Fresno Bee *and the* Sacramento Bee.

Standing outside the entrance to the Rainbow Ballroom, Karen Lee and Pa Xiong wait anxiously in the night for their friends. From where the two Clovis High School sopho-mores stand outside the downtown Fresno [California] dance hall, they can hear the music, talking and laughter inside. They want to join the party, but their friends haven't arrived yet.

"They're good," says Karen, 16, of the evening's main at-traction, a Hmong band called Paradise. "[The music] is bet-ter. It makes sense. Teenagers, we understand it. We can listen to it like American music."

As a new generation of Hmong-Americans like Karen and Pa come of age in the central San Joaquin Valley, bands are trying to appeal to their audience's ever-changing tastes. Some have adapted, some have never had to change and others have stopped playing.

Nzong Xiong, "World of New Music: Hmong-Americans are Playing the Sounds of Their Own Experience," *The Fresno Bee*, March 16, 2000, p. E1. Copyright © 2000 The Dialog Corporation. Reproduced by permission.

And now some are trying to broaden their audience beyond Americans of Hmong heritage. They're encouraged by the boom in Latin music that's crossed over into the Anglo pop scene.

Mitch Herr, manager of the band Whyteshadows, says the appetite for Hmong bands' music outside the Hmong community is "getting better compared to two to five years ago. The market is open and wider."

Hmong Accept Changes in Musical Styles

At the same time, the Hmong community seems more accepting of new and different styles of music emerging from Hmong bands, he says. "There's a market for it now. I think there's a good chance, not only for Whyteshadows, but for any band to make it."

"It's like a revolution," says Long Her of Paradise. "Things are changing so quickly. The youth moved from something like rock to something more hip-hop."

Paradise, Whyteshadows and Voltage, which later changed its name to High Voltage, are examples of bands that are playing to those changing music trends within the Hmong community. And, in some cases, hoping to follow the Latin music example and move into America's musical mainstream.

High Voltage, one of the earliest Hmong bands in the United States, was formed by three friends, but its debut came as a surprise to Paul Long Lo, originally the drummer and now lead singer, and his bandmates. It happened at a party in Merced several years ago. "Nobody knew who we were," says Lo, 30, who lives in Lompoc. "We just wanted to play."

When the party band took a break, "We played 30 minutes and five songs and it turned out the 400 to 500 people there liked us better than the original band." So Lo and his friends got serious about their music and started touring cities with large Hmong populations: Fresno; Eau Claire and Madison in Wisconsin; Minnesota's twin cities, St. Paul and Minneapolis, and Morganton, N.C. The band expanded to six members as its popularity grew.

"The era we were introduced to the community, [people] wanted more from the bands," Lo says. "We had the right ingredients at the right time. It was techno, new wave. It was what people wanted at a party."

High Voltage started in the 1980s; since then it has produced six albums.

Some Bands Also Incorporate Dance

Singing mainly in Hmong, High Voltage is equally at ease with slow love ballads and songs with feet-moving dance music for young people. At parties, the band also sings a few traditional Laotian songs for parents in the crowd. "We like to grab the interest of everybody," Lo says.

The band hopes to have a new album by the end of the year. However, with members scattered all over the United States because of family and work obligations, practice and new albums are not easy to organize. But High Voltage's reputation and longevity still assure large crowds when it plays.

Paradise is a big draw, too. Their choreographed dance moves during intermission remind fans of the Backstreet Boys and 'N Sync, and set Paradise apart from other Hmong bands. Long Her, 19, who plays keyboard, says, "It's easy for a musician to play music, but to feel or move to your own music, it's not easy."

A group of friends started Paradise to stay out of trouble, says lead singer Ko Yang. "Back then, the gangs were pretty hot and there were a lot of problems in the community," says Yang, 29. But as the band began to get serious, members took lessons and "it evolved from there on."

Paradise has been around since the early 1990s, but it wasn't until a few years ago that the band's name began to make waves in the Hmong community. "When we started, we shot for a rock culture feel," Her says. When it didn't work, "we changed our music to more modern, more R&B music."

That worked. Paradise's fourth album, "Heavenly Sent," was released during the 2000 Hmong International New Year in Fresno, and another is due out before the year is over and there's a concert tour in the works, too. Songs, most of them with a hip-hop feel, are sung in Hmong, English and, occasionally, French.

While Paradise has been going steadily for about a decade, Whyteshadows won the band contest during the 1991 Fresno Hmong New Year, released its debut album in 1992, then didn't have a second album until last year.

"The band has been here for a long time, but back then we were still young," says Seah Fang, 22, who plays the keyboard and composes most of the music. "What really got us started was last year when we started our second album. Everyone's more settled now. They have the time to put in and work hard with the band."

Audience for Hmong Music Is Growing

And there's more of an audience. "Even though the Hmong market is small, it's better now than five years ago," says Mitch Herr, 29, who plays guitar and manages the six-member band. "In the past year, it's been very exciting," says singer Angela Fang, 22. "We didn't plan to sell that many albums. We didn't think anyone would buy it."

But the audience, primarily teens, like the pop flavor of Whyteshadows' music. And Hmong parents—like their counterparts in the rest of American society—are less concerned about chaperoning teens at parties.

"Ten years ago . . . girls had to go to parties with their parents and families," says Phong Yang, 27, who plays bass for Paradise. "Nowadays, you have 13- and 14-year-olds coming to parties and they're unsupervised. They're very independent now."

Paul Long Lo, would like to see some things less Americanized. "The Hmong music scene has [moved away] from our culture," he says. "We really need to do more songs about the Hmong people."

But the ultimate dream for many of Hmong bands is to hit it big in mainstream American music. "I think there's room for improvement," says Seah Fang, "but I think we've come a long way [and] that other nationalities are starting to take notice that the Hmong people have talent and music, too."

CHAPTER 4

COMING *TO*
AMERICA

Accomplished Hmong Americans

Vang Pao: War Veteran and Lobbyist

Tony Kennedy and Paul McEnroe

Vang Pao was recruited by the Central Intelligence Agency in the 1950s to help the United States fight a covert war in Laos. He was already well known for his courage and fierce fighting in World War II and in the French war against the North Vietnamese. Vang accepted the offer to fight the Communists for the United States and went on to lead a clandestine Hmong army until the United States pulled out of the war in Vietnam, abandoning Vang and his army without support. In this selection Tony Kennedy and Paul McEnroe describe Vang Pao, the end of the war, and his struggle to help the Hmong refugees enter Thailand and then immigrate to other countries around the world, including the United States. The authors describe Vang's often dark moods and his position as elder statesman for the Hmong in America. Vang's work, however, is steeped in controversy and some Hmong believe he has abandoned the Hmongs' real needs and assumed a thirst for money. Now Vang lives in Southern California and lobbies in Washington on behalf of Hmong immigrants.

Kennedy and McEnroe are staff reporters with the Minneapolis–St. Paul Star Tribune.

A Legacy In Question

Just before the Vietnam War, the CIA hand-picked a charismatic Hmong officer to lead a covert war in Laos. His loyalty paved the way for Hmong to immigrate to the United States. For years he has asked his people to give money to overthrow the Communists in their homeland. His operations have attracted investigators in Minnesota and elsewhere.

Tony Kennedy and Paul McEnroe, "The Covert Wars of Vang Pao," *Star Tribune*, July 2, 2005. Copyright © Cowles Media Co. 2005. Reproduced with permission of Star Tribune, Minneapolis-St. Paul.

Vang Pao rode shotgun, his CIA man in the rear seat. Their single-engine plane, buffeted by strong crosswinds, aimed at a short dirt airstrip scratched into the face of a rocky northern Laotian mountain.

To Vang Pao, the Hmong warrior, there was little to worry about—divine spirits controlled his fate.

The plane landed near a village of about 300 people, defended by 60 men with old flintlock rifles, recalled Vinton Lawrence, the CIA operative.

Pathet Lao Communists let loose almost immediately with gunfire and mortar. "Instead of cowering, Vang Pao was up, directing these poor people who hadn't even been trained," Lawrence said of that day in the early 1960s. "His reaction was extraordinary. He assumed he was not going to get shot. He just exuded bravery."

It seemed he'd always lived this way.

As a teenager, Vang Pao had fought the Japanese in World War II, and in the 1950s he fought under the French in their disastrous war against the North Vietnamese.

In the late 1950s, when the CIA's Bill Lair was looking for someone to lead a covert war in Laos, Vang Pao's name kept coming up. Here was a soldier's soldier, Lair thought. The first one into battle and the last one out. In 1961, he asked Vang Pao the question: Would he fight the Communists for the United States?

The man from the hills didn't hesitate: Give him weapons and he would fight. Lair had his man.

Today, 30 years after the war, Vang Pao's reputation as a warrior has been cast aside and his legacy is in doubt. There are those who claim that the Hmong people he defended in Laos he later exploited in the United States.

Vang Pao had first attracted the CIA's attention because of his courage and the way he understood the political structures of the tribal clans. He mixed pride, fear, patronage and inspirational talk to motivate villages to follow him. He married for politics as well as for love, taking wives from different clans to unify his forces.

He rose to the rank of general and became a revered and honored figure in the Hmong world and a person of influence in the United States, associating with civic leaders, military officials and members of Congress.

Because of Vang Pao, tens of thousands of Hmong were able to immigrate to the United States after the war. Today, more than 350,000 Hmong live in America, nearly 60,000 of them in Minnesota. This weekend, more than 20,000 Hmong from across the country are expected to attend the 25th annual Hmong soccer festival in St. Paul's Como Park. It's not known whether Vang Pao will attend.

In late 2003 and into 2004, a tumultuous political split occurred between the general and many of his former soldiers. The split was followed by violence—a rowdy demonstration and unsolved shootings and fire-bombings in the St. Paul Hmong community, including the arson destruction of the home Vang Pao often stayed in.

Meanwhile, bitterness grows in the Hmong community over decades of aggressive fundraising by Neo Hom, the general's vast and secretive operation. Even one of Vang Pao's admirers in the CIA questions Neo Hom, saying it raises funds based on the dubious premise that Vang Pao will someday lead the Hmong back to Laos to overthrow the Communists.

Aging Hmong immigrants, many say, have given untold millions of dollars to that cause. But now their American-born children question what happened to the money their parents and grandparents gave.

Vang Pao declined to be interviewed for this series. His son Cha Vang denied that Hmong have been pressured to contribute to Neo Hom. He said that his father has made tremendous sacrifices to help his people. "It's hurt him, his blood, to have someone attack us," Cha Vang said. "He'd give himself up in the ultimate sacrifice."

Some of Vang Pao's operations have attracted the attention of state and federal investigators. The FBI is investigating possible bribery attempts surrounding a new Hmong funeral home in St. Paul—once slated to be operated by the Vang Pao Foundation.

And more recently, the state attorney general's office has raised questions about the foundation's spending. A lawsuit alleges that it violated state charities laws and can't account for more than $500,000.

With the scandals and questions, Neo Hom is drying up. And with it, Vang Pao's currency as a leader has been devalued.

"The general needs to preserve and protect his legacy," said Lee Pao Xiong, director of Concordia University's Center for Hmong Studies in St. Paul. "When you open up a history book, you want to read about his heroics, not the scandals or the perceived scandals.

"But when things like this happen, you can't ignore it."

One Tough Guerrilla

To look at him now, there's no clue about his past ferocity. Well-manicured and sharply dressed in a suit and tie, Vang Pao—now in his 70s and living in California—was featured last year in a poster campaign by the Hennepin County Library encouraging Hmong children to read. Paunchy, balding and beaming in the photo, he held a Hmong version of "Cinderella."

The same man was depicted in a series of photos in 1965 taken by John Willheim, an American working in Laos. Those pictures showed him launching grenades, drawing up bombing plans and interrogating a crouching prisoner who was tied to a leash.

His power came from his personality as much as from his battlefield prowess.

"VP, when I first met him, I think he was probably the greatest guerrilla leader in the world," Lair said recently from his home in Texas. "He was very smart, and he knew how to talk. . . . He could almost make these little guys levitate with the strength of his speech."

Years later, CIA Director William Colby told Congress that Vang Pao's fight in Laos kept 70,000 North Vietnamese from deploying in South Vietnam to kill Americans. The war killed 35,000 of Vang Pao's countrymen, cost the United States more than $1 billion and reshaped the geopolitical landscape south of China.

To overtake South Vietnam and the Americans, vast numbers of North Vietnamese troops and supplies would have had to come through Laos. Vang Pao's guerrilla troops—fighting on the ground while overhead the United States conducted one of its largest bombing campaigns ever—ambushed and slaughtered them.

The general's loyalty to Washington paved the way for all Hmong immigration to America. It was payback for all of his years of carving into North Vietnamese Army divisions.

"He's the godfather who brought us all here," said Xang Vang, a St. Paul entrepreneur and confidant of the general.

There was no wonder that the Hmong were so devoted to Vang Pao.

A Big-Hearted Man

On an unremarkable day in a long war, the roar from two U.S. fighter jets grew louder. As the pilots neared what they thought was their enemy target in the green hills of Laos, Vang Pao watched as his soldiers braced for the bombs. The attack targeted North Vietnamese infantry heading south. But the pilots miscalculated.

The bombs rained down very close to where Vang Pao stood. Thunderous explosions shook the landscape to his left and his right, driving him to the ground.

Then, to his troops, a miracle: Vang Pao rose from the smoke and debris, unscathed.

The escape from death had a profound effect on him, his adviser, Steve Young, said years later. Vang Pao believed he survived for a reason.

Young said that Vang Pao told him, "I must have been saved by the spirits, by some reason to do good for my people."

That sense of duty drove him to be even more courageous. From the earliest days of the war, Ly Teng was one who witnessed Vang Pao's fearlessness.

Ly Teng, now 63 and a businessman in the Twin Cities, was once the chief of operations in Vang Pao's army. He is married to one of Vang Pao's sisters.

He can recount the time the general walked away from a plane crash, the time he survived getting shot in the chest and arm, and the times in the 1960s when Vang Pao fought off two attempted coups by Hmong factions.

While the names of individual battles and the exploits of men have blurred over time, what remains clear to Ly Teng is the code that the general pounded into his troops.

"His words were, 'If we die, we die together. Nobody will be left behind,'" Teng said. "He never commanded from headquarters. Every day he was with his soldiers. He knew the soldiers were paid very little, so he would always share what food he had with them. They saw he was a regular guy, a very fair man. We called him 'Siab Loj.' A big hearted man."

Dark Moods

It was, in the early years, the kind of war that made Vinton Lawrence feel as though he'd never been more alive. He watched C-130s on midnight runs dropping M-1 rifles and mortars in the middle of the jungle and made sure Vang Pao's men got them.

Vang Pao and his men taught him how to live off the land. Their meals were sometimes supplemented by food rations airdropped by the United States—once, leftovers from the Bay of Pigs Cuban operation: beans and Spanish rice. During hit-and-run operations, Vang Pao's men showed him how to eat on the fly—wrap some rice in a banana leaf and go.

Lawrence was 21 when, as a CIA operative working under Bill Lair, he was sent into Laos in February 1962 to work with Vang Pao from his base in Long Cheng. About 10 years younger than Vang Pao, Lawrence became like a son to the Hmong leader.

"I saw him under all kinds of situations and I was deeply impressed by his altruism, and to the extent he saw beyond the borders of Laos," Lawrence said recently. "He was a very, very impressive leader."

While Vang Pao exuded charisma, Lawrence saw what few were allowed to see. "I saw his dark moods when things were not going well," he said. "The dark moods came when he rubbed up against the corruption of the Lao government because he realized that no matter how hard he tried and how heroic he was, there were going to be Lao who would never accept him."

The commander's reputation carried to the leaders of the most elite forces in the world. Retired U.S. Air Force Brig. Gen. Harry (Heinie) Aderholt, who ran a covert operation in Laos during the war, saw how the outnumbered Hmong were willing to fight for Vang Pao.

"He was the only person capable of leading the Hmong forces," Aderholt recalled recently. "Without his devotion, his talent, the Hmong would have gone under years ago."

To this day, Aderholt considers Vang Pao to have been the top general in Southeast Asia at the time. "Better than any American general over there," he said.

Aderholt said that whenever one of Vang Pao's units was struggling to take a position, the general would intervene, inspiring his soldiers to the point where "they'd go up that mountain at any cost."

Lawrence said that Vang Pao had come to peace with the prospect of dying. "When we talked about it, he said, 'Look, God has a ticket for me; if it's going to be my time it's going to be my time.'"

The CIA's Lair still marvels at the finesse of Vang Pao's hit-and-run army. In the mountain terrain, the North Vietnamese were no match for Vang Pao's irregulars as long as they stuck to their guerrilla tactics, he said.

"You'd almost swear they must have helicopters to move that fast," Lair said.

His Growing Influence

Vang Pao also had a dark side that has been chronicled in scholarly books. He was rumored to traffic in opium, using planes provided by the CIA to export the drugs out of the country. One such book, *Harvesting Pa Chay's Wheat*, alleges that Vang Pao turned to narcotics in order to pay his troops after CIA funding stopped in 1974. Vang Pao has denied accusations of drug dealing in the past.

Lair said he has seen things that Vang Pao has done that could, by some, be considered barbaric. "When I first got up there, when they captured prisoners—both sides did it—they automatically killed all the prisoners," he said.

But to Lair, context is everything. Troops on both sides killed their prisoners because it was nearly impossible to confine them securely in the jungle, he said.

"I talked to him [Vang Pao] about it. I said, 'Look, when you capture these guys, we ought not to shoot 'em 'cause they know a lot of stuff; we can get information out of 'em which would be very useful to us,'" Lair said. "He wasn't shooting them because he was a barbarian. He didn't know what else to do with them."

In time, Lair said, Vang Pao tried to persuade prisoners to join his army and sometimes carried out a rescue mission to retrieve a prisoner's family from behind enemy lines, thereby ensuring the prisoner would remain loyal to him.

In recruiting Hmong soldiers, Vang Pao was known to spread money and goods in villages where loyalty was strong. If a village rejected his recruiting efforts, it might be left unprotected against enemy attack.

Aderholt said Vang Pao was only being true to his role as a guerrilla chieftain.

"Vang Pao's a son of a bitch, but he's our son of a bitch," Aderholt said.

"Everybody was afraid of him. They had reason to."

Toward the end of the war, Lair said, Vang Pao had many admirers back in Washington. "Big leaders, generals and big people from the State Department, all kinds of people came and visited him and promised him all sorts of things," Lair said.

With the attention came meddling from the Americans. Vang Pao's strength was in his army's mobility. He was outnumbered and didn't have enough men to hold positions on every mountain. But he could sweep his territory of the North Vietnamese before they became entrenched.

As criticism of the Vietnam War increased, however, the Americans pressured Vang Pao to abandon his guerrilla attacks and engage the North Vietnamese in more traditional warfare. The new initiative to increase body counts came from higher-ups who hoped to deceive the public into thinking that the United States was winning the war because more North Vietnamese were dying, Lair said.

But this kind of combat decimated the Hmong ranks.

"When they stood and fought toe to toe with the Vietnamese infantry, they would lose, and lose a lot of people," Lair said.

Vang Pao found himself leading an army of kids—young teens who were filling in behind men who had died in the war.

According to Lair and Ly Teng, Vang Pao's biggest miscalculation was off the battlefield. He believed that he would never lose U.S. backing. He didn't understand that Americans were growing sick of Vietnam and that the political winds were shifting.

"I talked to him in 1973 after I saw the news talking about a U.S. pullout," Ly Teng recalled. "I said, 'We need to be careful.'

"He told me, 'Don't worry about that; we've worked too hard for that to happen.' He trusted America very much. He thought America would never leave him behind."

The Bloody End

Rousted from his sleep, the veteran fighter pilot reached in the darkness for the phone ringing in his room in Vientiane, the Laotian capital. Jack Knotts was used to plans made on the run, especially in these waning days of a war being lost. Within minutes, he understood how badly events up north were unraveling.

An Air Force special operations officer told him that he and Heinie Aderholt had just finished drawing up the secret plans for "an extraction."

Get up to Long Cheng—Vang Pao's headquarters hundreds of miles to the north—by dawn, Knotts was ordered. It was May 14, 1975.

Knotts had flown fighter jets in World War II, served in South Vietnam and then worked in Laos, flying for Air America, the CIA's covert air transport company. Now he was working out of the Laotian capital as a helicopter pilot. He was confident he could navigate any mountaintop or ravine from the China border to the Mekong River bordering South Vietnam.

For the past few weeks, North Vietnamese and Pathet Lao troops had steadily advanced on the Hmong's last military base. Tens of thousands of Hmong had fled their mountain villages.

A few U.S. transport planes would airlift out as many of the refugees as possible. Knotts anticipated a scene similar to the one a month earlier when Saigon had fallen: families with crying children being dragged into overloaded planes straining to take off.

That kind of chaos, Knotts had been told, would serve as the cover needed to pull off the last U.S. mission in Laos—the rescue of Gen. Vang Pao.

Vang Pao was to be "extracted," while most of his loyal soldiers—teenagers and middle-aged men—would be left behind. The commander who had always been the last off a battlefield was, under CIA orders, being pressured to break one of his most fervently upheld rules.

"VP could not be seen getting into an aircraft on the runway with thousands and thousands of Hmong people around. It had to be done secretly," Knotts said recently, now 81 and recounting the tale by phone from his home in Florida.

When Knotts, in his helicopter, and fellow pilot Dave Kouba, flying his small Porter airplane, arrived in Long Cheng at 6:30 a.m., they saw more than 20,000 people strung along the airstrip. C-46 transport planes were soon flying in to start the evacuation. "It was crazy that day," Knotts said. "You know how word gets around. You could tell from the crowd . . . they thought they were gonna get their heads chopped off. It was like panic. Like Saigon on the last day."

Knotts and Kouba walked into a stone building. Soon after, Vang Pao entered and was briefed. Behind a residence known as the King's House, a ridgeline ran parallel to the runway. Behind it was a large fish pond with an earthen dam.

The plan called for Knotts to circle out of sight of the runway at a spot called Checkpoint Peter. When Vang Pao signaled, Knotts would fly over to the dam and pick him up.

Knotts would drop Vang Pao off at another location and then go back to pick up Jerry Daniels, Vang Pao's CIA confidant. Kouba would then fly both men to Thailand.

"VP, being reluctant to leave, was dragging his heels a little bit," Knotts said. "And I have to say Jerry was doing not much better. It was wrenching for him, too. He'd been there for years."

By now, it was past 10 a.m. Knotts took off. After feinting one way for several miles, he turned south and headed back for Checkpoint Peter. From about 2,000 feet he looked down and saw a flash. Vang Pao's signal glinted in the sun.

Knotts landed on the dam. "And VP was there with his son. He's got a camouflage outfit, uniform-like, a baseball cap with some 'scrambled eggs' on the top; the son had a big weapon. There was no conversation. We said hello to one another and that's about it. Oh, God, he was sad."

Knotts dropped off the general and his son at an abandoned airstrip, then headed back to pick up Daniels, the last American left in Laos.

Daniels stood "with his back to me and the helicopter, and he looked up at the sky and came to rigid attention and he gave a salute," Knotts said. "There were tears. This is the end, the bloody end."

As Knotts and Daniels flew in, Knotts looked down and saw Vang Pao surrounded by a crowd of refugees who, like him, were on the run. "He was handing out what money he had," Knotts said. "He was passing out all the money he had in his hand to the people."

By day's end, Vang Pao was in Thailand, and within months he would be living in America. But he wasn't about to give up his warrior past.

Mee Moua: Member of State Congress

Mee Moua

Mee Moua is the first Hmong American woman to become elected to Minnesota State Congress. Moua came to the United States with her family in 1978 and worked her way up from the public housing projects of Appleton, Wisconsin, to become a legislator in the state capitol of St. Paul, Minnesota, in 2002. Moua is also an accomplished attorney who lives with her mother, her husband, and their two children. In this selection Moua describes how she grew up in Laos and Thailand, emigrating to America when she was nine years old. She describes what it was like to live in a strange land, where the customs are extremely different from her homeland's. She also underscores the importance of education and details her decision to run for the legislature. She states that she is proud of the contributions Asian Americans are making in the political arena.

I was born in a remote village in Laos in 1969. When I was five, my family left for the refugee camps in Thailand and in 1978, when I was 9, we came to the U.S. I don't remember Laos, but I remember Ban Vinai refugee camp in Thailand.

As a child, the camp was lots of fun. I think they tried to set up a school, but there were no consistent classes. It was just a long period of playtime. There were always adults around and we would all listen to them tell stories.

The UNHCR [United Nations Refugee Agency] brought the refugees food rations and I remember standing in line for food. I remember feeling like we couldn't eat as much as we needed to and sometimes the meat was already rotten. But still, our family was better off because my father had a job as a medic and we could supplement what wasn't enough.

Life in the US

First, we went to Providence, Rhode Island. We were fortunate because we came in the summer. I can't imagine how the families who came during the winter adjusted from the heat of Southeast Asia to the cold of North America.

I remember our first night at the apartment, my mom was trying to learn how to use the gas stove, the taps. We had seen toilets before, but we had to get used to just pushing a button to flush the toilet instead of bringing in buckets of water.

Our sponsors gave us a sheet set and my mom used one fitted sheet for one bed, and the flat sheet on another bed, and knotted the ends to keep it on the bed. I remember feeling like I had no clue what was going on.

We stayed in Rhode Island for seven months, then we moved to Appleton, Wisconsin, where we stayed until I graduated from high school.

Hmong in the Mid-West

In Appleton, everyone was white and all their last names started with Van, or they had names like Johnson. Everyone was Catholic. I remember when my parents became citizens. They asked if we wanted to change our names and I asked my parents if we could add Van to our name so I could be Mee Van Moua. They vetoed that idea! Anyway, I kept my Hmong name and most of my siblings did, except my brother Mang, who changed his name to Mike.

There were a couple of Filipino families, they were doctors and researchers at [the company] Kimberly-Clark, so they were very privileged and they didn't identify with us. We were minorities and we were also really poor. We lived in a public housing duplex and everyone knew we were the poor.

Church people would show up at our house on Christmas with trees and stuff, but there were also people who spit at us and called us chinks, gooks and told us to go home. The hostility was so overt that it made us feel very different, so my siblings and I became very rooted in our Hmongness.

A Background for Politics

Initially my intention was to become a doctor, what Asian family doesn't want their child to become a doctor, right? But when I was at Brown [University], I got involved in protests and I felt very empowered. I learned a new language and for the first time, I was able to identify racism and I learned about pluralism. I felt smart, creative and I thought, "Wow, I'm doing something that makes a difference."

I majored in public policy and we studied welfare, poverty, social security, Medicare—all the things I was familiar with because I spent years filling out forms for my family.

In my junior year, I became a Junior Fellow at Princeton and I also got a Woodrow Wilson fellowship to study public policy at the University of Texas, Austin. In 1997, I came home to attend law school at the University of Minnesota.

In Minnesota, I worked on my Uncle Neal Thaos' campaign for the St. Paul School Board. I learned a lot about how to run a campaign and about the nuts and bolts of the political process. I also met lots of candidates and many of them encouraged me to run for office. So the seeds were planted.

I hadn't really planned to run now [2002], but a Senate seat was vacant. It seemed like the right opportunity, the right time. Being the first Hmong woman to be elected to the State Senate has brought pride to the Hmong community. I think it marks a turning point in the community.

The Asian American Political Landscape

Asian American politicians could do more, but we have made great headway in many states. Satveer Chaudhary was elected to the Minnesota House of Representatives in 1996. Until his election, no Asian American has ever been elected to the Minnesota Legislature. Between 1996 and 2003, there have been three representatives in the legislature, two in the Senate and one in the House, so we've made a lot of progress. It's put the state of Minnesota on the map.

There's also been progress in other states such as Michigan, Wisconsin, Arkansas and Iowa. So, now Asian American politicians are no longer only in the East or the West Coast but in states that have not previously had a strong Asian American presence.

I am tremendously excited about Asian Americans in politics and we're poised to move to the next level. There is a sense of excitement that this is our time. My generation of young politicians has graduated from Japanese Americans to Chinese Americans to more Filipino Americans, Korean Americans, Korean adoptees, Southeast Asian Americans and Asian Indians.

The issue is not whether the Asian American politicians are ready, it's really whether America is ready.

Tou Ger Xiong: Rapper and Comedian

Nzong Xiong

Tou Ger Xiong was born in Laos in 1973. Xiong's father served with the CIA, and his family was forced to flee Laos after the Communist takeover in 1975. After four years in a Thai refugee camp, Xiong's family immigrated to the United States as refugees of war. Journalist Nzong Xiong describes in this next selection how Tou Ger Xiong developed a passion for the performance arts and created Project Respectism, an educational service project that uses comedy, storytelling, and rap music to bridge cultures and generations. Tou Ger Xiong presented his project to schools, churches, libraries, colleges, and community groups throughout the Midwest. Project Respectism has since evolved into a program that provides cultural entertainment and education for people of all professions and backgrounds, Nzong Xiong writes.

Nzong Xiong is a contributing journalist for newspapers including the Fresno Bee *and the* Sacramento Bee.

During one of Tou Ger Xiong's early performances to a group of young and old Hmong, he came to a stunning realization describing to the audience his immigrant father's struggle to assimilate into American society.

"You could see all these faces. They were red—people wiping tears—and their eyes were glued onto me," Xiong remembers. "Then I started laughing, and I got them to laugh. Afterward, I said, 'Wow.' That day, I saw I had a gift."

It was an emotional moment for Xiong, 26, a comedian, rapper and actor from St. Paul, Minn. . . .

Xiong immigrated to the United States in 1979 when he was 6 years old. He began performing during his senior year in high school as part of a mentoring program.

Nzong Xiong, "Gift Rap: This Child of the Hmong Culture Has a Message about Being Human," *The Fresno Bee*, May 4, 2000, p. E1. Copyright © 2000 The Dialog Corporation. Reproduced by permission.

As a child growing up in the Twin Cities of St. Paul and Minneapolis, Xiong heard ethnic slurs and people telling him, "Go back to your own country."

Then, he says, there was just plain ignorance of the Hmong people: "People would come up to me and say, 'What are you?'" Xiong recalls.

Project Respectism

During his third year as a political science student at Carleton College in Northfield, Minn., he created "Project Respectism," an educational service project mixing comedy, storytelling and rap music to bridge cultures and generations. The project evolved into a program today that entertains and educates people of all backgrounds and professions.

In audiences of Hmong speakers and people who don't speak Hmong, Xiong easily switches between Hmong and English. He might start a joke in Hmong, then quickly translate in such a way that the translation seems like part of the act. "It's a very unique balance," says Xiong, one of 11 siblings. "It's not hard. At first it was, but after a while you learn to connect with the different people."

Xiong believes it is important for him to reach communities where there are no Hmong people. "I go there saying we're different, but we have no choice but to get along," he says. "I try to get away from the political issues and try to remind everybody we're all human beings."

Getting the audience involved in his rap is part of Xiong's communication initiative. He decided to go with rap as a medium to relate to youth. "I have more of an impact if I'm talking in the language of the youth," he says. "Not that they won't learn anything if I'm wearing a suit and tie and giving a lecture, but I want to build rapport." He often gets his audiences, young and old, chanting: "Go Hmong boy. Go Hmong boy. Go!"

Like many comedians, Xiong gets material from his own experiences. "It's a reflection of my life and the Hmong life in America" that includes "everyday interaction of being Hmong, how we eat, how we prepare our food, our cultural traditions and the struggles of having to live in two worlds," he says.

Xiong's Program Celebrates the Hmong

Over the past few years, Xiong has given more than 500 presentations and visited nearly 30 states. Now he wants to write a book and further his acting career.

Traveling has given him the chance to see progress occurring in Hmong communities throughout the United States. "We're moving beyond refugee [status] and . . . into this new American community," he says. "I've met Hmong doctors, business owners, police officers, inventors, musicians, artists. I'm proud of all these people. We're making strides. We've come a long way."

Among the people Xiong talks about in his act are the people who came to the United States first. . . . "This is a wonderful opportunity to celebrate our refugee elders," says the Rev. Sharon Stanley, executive director of FIRM [Fresno Interdenominational Refugee Ministries]. "The program is organized to raise awareness of their strengths and needs. The stories Tou Ger tells about immigration magnifies those of the elders."

Xa Xiong: Doctor

Wendy Harris

When Xa Xiong lived with his family in a refugee camp in Thailand, he made a promise to himself. As Xiong's brother lay dying with no help from medicines or doctors, Xiong vowed he would one day become a doctor. Many years later in America, Xiong fulfilled his dream of becoming a doctor. Now working in the Fox Cities area of Wisconsin, Xiong has another dream: to help other doctors understand how to work more effectively with Hmong patients. In this selection journalist Wendy Harris describes Xiong's medical practice and his work helping the Western medical community learn to be more compassionate and respectful of the traditions of the Hmong immigrants. Xiong helps doctors learn about Hmong customs and beliefs and also focuses on treating elderly Hmong patients.

Harris is a feature reporter for the Post-Crescent *in Appleton, Wisconsin.*

When Xa Xiong was a boy, he made a seemingly impossible promise during a tragic time. As his older brother, Pao Xiong, lay dying in Thailand's Bin Vinai refugee camp, Xiong pledged he would become a doctor.

The promise seemed as far-fetched as his family's return to their home in Laos, from which they fled in May 1975 after the fall of Saigon. It was a promise that Xiong, 36, now the first Hmong doctor in the Fox Cities [Wisconsin], would keep.

Xiong was 7 when his father smuggled his mom, four siblings and about 150 other refugees across the Mekong River to the camp. While it protected them from the Viet Cong, it did not keep them safe from disease.

"I watched him close his eyes and take his last breath," said Xiong, a first-year resident in the University of Wisconsin's

Wendy Harris, "Hmong Doctor Bridges the Culture Gap," *The Post-Crescent*, July 19, 2005. Reproduced by permission.

Fox Valley Family Medicine Residency Program in Appleton. "I made up my mind at that time to become a doctor."

Xiong also lost a little sister in the camp. There was no doctor, no antibiotics, no medical examiner to determine the causes of death. Xiong suspects his siblings died of malaria or pneumonia.

Xiong Comes to America

Xiong and his family emigrated to California in 1980, when Xiong enrolled in school. "I remember people making fun of me when I started to speak English," he recalls. That only strengthened his resolve to succeed.

Xiong holds a bachelor's degree in biology, a doctor of chiropractic degree and a medical degree. "I'm not just looking forward to working for my own community, but everyone in town," he said.

Xiong will spend the next three years working toward his board certification in family medicine. As part of the training, Xiong will serve as a physician at the UW Health Fox Valley Family Practice.

Xiong is one of four Hmong doctors in Wisconsin, which is home to roughly 50,000 Hmong residents. Xiong, already nationally known and sought after, decided to settle in the area with his wife and five children. That is welcome news to both the region's Hmong and health care communities.

"I'm very excited about this and am very happy that he decided to move to the Fox Cities to do his residency," said Lo Lee, executive director of Appleton's Hmong American Partnership.

"He's a really wonderful human being and we are glad he has this opportunity with us," said Dr. Lee Vogel, campus director of the Appleton-based family residency program.

Xiong Begins His Practice

Xiong moved here from Madison, where his wife and children remain. They are used to being apart, and are grateful there is only a two-hour drive separating them.

Xiong attended medical school in the Caribbean and later did internships in Mexico, Arizona and Alaska. His wife, Choua Yang, stayed in Santa Ana, Calif., working as an accountant and raising their children. "My wife has a big heart and she has sacrificed a lot of her time putting me through school," Xiong said.

For the past two years, Xiong worked with elderly Hmong clients of Kajsiab House, part of the mental health center of Dane County. It gave him an appreciation for geriatric care, something he hopes to emphasize as a doctor.

In addition to serving the Hmong community, Xiong also hopes to bridge the gap between Hmong culture and Western medicine by educating physicians on Hmong customs and beliefs. Language barriers aside, Western physicians can easily offend their Hmong patients, and likewise, Hmong traditions can seem a little unusual to uninformed doctors.

Xiong Works to Educate Physicians

For example, it's inappropriate to ask a Hmong family that has lost [a] loved one whether the deceased wanted to be an organ donor. "In the Hmong culture, if someone dies, we like to keep every tissue and organ in the body," he said. "It's a very sensitive issue and my suggestion to (doctors) is that you don't walk in and ask 'would you like to donate the organs to other people?'"

The taboo is based on the Hmong belief that if people lose their vital organs after death, they cannot be reborn into a new body.

Doctors also need to be sensitive to Hmong patients when blood tests are performed. "The Hmong believe that when you drain the blood there is no replenishment," Xiong said.

Additionally, Xiong knows better than to ever compliment a Hmong baby, no matter how adorable or cute the child is. The Hmong believe that babies are born with multiple life souls that can become easily separated from their bodies.

Predatory dabs, or evil spirits, they believe, have been known to steal souls and make babies sick. So the Hmong are careful not to call attention to their babies.

While many Hmong beliefs are rooted in thousands of years of history, some traditions are having to adapt to Western influence—like burying a baby's placenta.

The Hmong believe that when someone dies, the soul retraces its life path back [to] the burial place of its placenta. Xiong says doctors shouldn't be surprised if a Hmong woman asks to take the baby's placenta home.

Bill Yang: Entrepreneur

Sheryl Jean

After he was laid off from his computer job, Hmong immigrant Bill Yang decided to create his own business, a Web development and computer-consulting firm called Hmongmedia Interactive. He is one of a handful of Hmong computer business owners in St. Paul, Minnesota. In this selection journalist Sheryl Jean describes the early days of Hmongmedia and how Yang has built his successful business. Yang sees his biggest challenge as building credentials to attract larger, more mainstream customers. Jean also reports Yang's newest vision of networking Hmong businesses together in an effort to bring prosperity to more Hmong lives.

Jean is a staff writer for the St. Paul Pioneer Press *in St. Paul, Minnesota.*

Bill Yang didn't plan to be a pioneering Hmong entrepreneur, but that's what happened when he lost his job three years ago.

Hmongmedia Interactive, the Web development and computer-consulting firm he started, is one of a handful of Hmong-owned technology companies in Minnesota. The company's specialty is interactive Web sites.

"If it wasn't for the layoff, I wouldn't be doing this," said Bill Yang, who started the company in his basement. "It's a lot of small, gradual steps. Everything is falling into place."

He's also on a mission to help advance the Hmong community by working on projects with other entrepreneurs and employing young people. His long-term goal is to have enough capital and resources to develop interactive educational software for Hmong children to learn about their ethnic background.

Sheryl Jean, "Widening the Web," *St. Paul Pioneer Press*, July 25, 2004. Republished with permission of St. Paul Pioneer Press, conveyed through Copyright Clearance Center, Inc.

"Many of our clients are Hmong small businesses," he said. "We go in as brothers and sisters to help them build their businesses."

Like many small businesses, Hmongmedia has experienced its share of ups and downs. Bill Yang, 33, brought in distant relative Fong Yang, 38, as his partner last spring after going through three other partners who didn't share the same vision. The company also has faced family issues—Bill Yang has struggled with day care for his four children ages 3 to 9—and growth and funding issues.

Bill Yang and Fong Yang each initially invested $5,000 in the business, and they have sacrificed salaries so far. Their spouses' full-time jobs support the families while the men build the business. They credit small-business training at the nonprofit Neighborhood Development Center in St. Paul with helping them establish a strong foundation.

The company's 2004 revenue is estimated at about $60,000. Hmongmedia's main goal this year is to make a profit, Bill Yang said.

Humble Beginnings in Laos

Both entrepreneurs, who were born in Laos, are experienced at taking risks. An ethnic minority, the Hmong fought in a CIA-backed campaign against Communists in Laos during the Vietnam War. When the Communists took control in 1975, many Hmong fled to the United States.

At age 5, Bill Yang and his family moved to Eau Claire, Wis., from Laos, among the first wave of Hmong immigrants around 1975. Fong Yang joined Bill Yang's family in Wisconsin in 1978, and his parents followed two years later. They moved several times before settling in St. Paul.

Both partners got hooked on computers at an early age. Bill Yang most recently worked at Cdxc Corp. in St. Paul, but he also has worked as a tech supporter or software engineer at 3M Co., HealthPartners and Veritas Software Corp. Fong Yang has been a systems administrator at Htech Group in St. Paul, a support technician for Tires Plus and a sales engineer at National Business Systems.

Hmongmedia has about 150 customers, mainly Hmong businesses such as Hmong Times and Hmong Today. Bill Yang first wanted to gain the support of the Hmong community and some of the largest Hmong businesses. The company has several non-Hmong customers, such as Fantom Optics in Golden Valley and Lynn R. Schwartz Photography in St. Paul.

"What we wanted was someone who could build the (Web) engine and leave it flexible enough for us to work with," said Harry Miller, president of start-up Fantom Optics, whose main product is a custom eyeglass clip-on called FantomClip. "They came through with it quickly, and price-wise they were competitive." Hmongmedia's price was 20 percent to 40 percent less than other companies, Miller said. Hmongmedia charges $500 to $3,000 to build a Web site.

Tackling the Challenge of Growth

The partners see their biggest challenge as building their credentials to attract larger, more mainstream customers. They're considering a new company name to reflect a broader focus and maybe keeping Hmongmedia as a division. One option is IB Technologies. IB means "one" in Hmong.

Last month, Hmongmedia moved to a larger office in a building with an elevator partly to portray a more professional appearance and to provide wheelchair access for newly hired Web developer Bing Xiong, who is a quadriplegic.

The partners are working with Dale White, a business consultant at the Neighborhood Development Center, to analyze their cash flow for the next two to three years and determine what sources of financing they might need to support growth plans. Hmongmedia would like to increase its staff of four and upgrade its equipment.

"The business is in a growth mode," White said. "Typically, growing businesses start to outrun their capital. These guys have taken a proactive approach to this by looking at how to structure their cash flow."

The number of Hmong businesses has grown and diversified in the past several years—from mainly small Asian food stores to auto sales, insurance and technology, said Chengny Thao, chairwoman of the Hmong Chamber of Commerce in St. Paul. Hmongmedia hosts the chamber's Web site.

"Like any immigrant group, you spend the first couple of years acclimating to the culture and the values," Chengny Thao said. "As you learn from the people around, you start to branch out."

Chronology

1810-1840

Many Hmong migrate out of China to Northern Laos by way of Vietnam, Burma, and Thailand.

1893

The French establish a protectorate over Laos.

1896

Hmong revolt over French taxes.

1919

The Hmong conduct the Mad Man's War in opposition to the French. They are unsuccessful, but the French decide to upgrade the Hmong political status.

1940

Japanese invade Laos, forcing French soldiers to hide in Hmong caves.

1941-1945

World War II is known to the Hmong as Rog Yivpoos—the "Japanese War." As WWII comes to an end, the French resume control of Laos.

1946

The cold war begins.

1946-1954

After the Japanese defeat in WWII, the Hmong help French fight Vietnamese invaders.

1950

European missionaries create the first modern Hmong written language. Vang Pao, a Hmong military officer, is recruited to spy for the French.

1954

Laos gains independence from France and becomes a member of the United Nations.

1959

American Green Berets begin training Hmong in Laos to fight Communist forces in the region.

1960

The United States enlists Vang Pao to lead nine thousand Hmong troops to fight the "secret war" in Laos. The Americans promise the Hmong arms, training, and food in the short run, and U.S. protection if things go poorly. At this time an estimated five hundred thousand Hmong live in Laos.

1962

Laos becomes officially neutral in the Vietnam War. The Geneva Accords places strict limits on U.S. participation in the Communist struggle in Southeast Asia.

1963-1975

The Vietnam War and the U.S. "secret war" in Laos are conducted.

1963

The Kennedy Administration authorizes the CIA to increase its secret Hmong army to twenty thousand.

1964

Vang Pao is named a general in the Royal Lao Army.

1965

The United States steps up the "secret war" in Laos by providing air support.

1967

The United States installs air guidance equipment in Laos. The Hmong continue to resist the Pathet Lao.

1968

U.S. pilots average three hundred sorties a day over Laos to battle 110,000 Communist troops.

1969-1970

Hmong save many U.S. pilots that were shot down over the Ho Chi Minh trail. Congress learns of the "secret war" in Laos for the first time. More than eighteen thousand Hmong have already died.

1973-74

U.S. pilots and support troops are pulled out of Laos, leaving the Hmong to battle more than forty thousand North Vietnamese troops without any support or protection.

1975

Laos falls to the Communists. The Americans complete their withdrawal from Southeast Asia. The Pathet Lao take control of Laos. More than thirty thousand Hmong die fleeing Laos. General Vang Pao and many of his officers are airlifted from Thailand by the U.S military. In retaliation for Hmong assistance to the United States, the Pathet Lao uses chemical weapons against the Hmong, killing an unreported number. In Thailand, more than a hundred thousand Hmong are forced to move to refugee camps.

1975

The first 3,466 Hmong refugees arrive in the United States.

1978

A second wave of immigration of Hmong to the United States begins. The Pathet Lao drops a chemical agent called "Yellow Rain" on Hmong villages in Laos.

1980

United Nations adopts a resolution to investigate the use of chemical-biological warfare in Laos, Cambodia, and Afghanistan. Another hundred thousand Hmong flee to Thailand. U.S. Congress passes the 1980 Refugee Act creating the Federal Refugee Resettlement Program to provide for the effective resettlement of refugees and to assist them to achieve economic self-sufficiency as quickly as possible after arrival in the United States.

1981

Scientists for the United Nations confirm that the Pathet Lao did use chemical weapons against the Hmong in Laos.

1985

The Thai government begins to repatriate Hmong refugees to Laos.

1990

Hmong refugees in the United States total about a hundred thousand.

1991

Laos, Thailand, and the United Nations sign an agreement to repatriate Hmong refugees to Laos.

1993

Hmong refugees flee Thai refugee camps rather than be repatriated.

1995

The Thai refugee camps are closed. Thousands of Hmong return to Laos, from which there are continuing reports of torture, persecution, and death.

1997

Hmong veterans are finally recognized in Washington, D.C., for their efforts during the Vietnam War.

2000

The U.S. Congress passes the U.S. Immigrant Act of 2000 making it easier for Hmong immigrants to obtain American citizenship. Census Bureau reports 169,000 Hmong live in the United States. Hmong guerrillas continue fighting in the mountains of northern Laos.

2003

The U.S. State Department announces the resettlement of fifteen thousand Hmong refugees from the Wat Tham Krabok refugee camp in Thailand.

For Further Research

Books

Mervyn Brown, *War in Shangri-La: A Memoir of Civil War in Laos*. New York: St. Martin's Press, 2001.

Sucheng Chan, *Hmong Means Free: Life in Laos and America*. Philadelphia: Temple University Press, 1994.

Kenneth Conboy, *Shadow War: The CIA's Secret War in Laos*. Boulder, CO: Paladin, 1995.

Kathleen A. Culhane-Pera, Dorothy E. Vawter, Phua Xiong, Barbara Babbitt, and Mary M. Solberg, eds., *Healing by Heart: Clinical and Ethical Case Stories of Hmong Families and Western Providers*. Nashville, TN: Vanderbilt University Press, 2003.

Robert Curry, *Whispering Death: Our Journey with the Hmong in the Secret War in Laos*. iUniverse, 2004.

Jin Dan and Ma Xueliang, eds., *Butterfly Mother: Miao Hmong Creation Epics from Guizhou, China*. Trans. Mark Bender. Indianapolis: Hackett, 2006.

Daniel F. Detzner, *Elder Voices: Southeast Asian Families in the United States*. Walnut Creek, CA: AltaMira, 2004.

Lillian Faderman, *I Begin My Life All Over: The Hmong and the American Immigrant Experience*. Boston: Beacon, 1999.

Anne Fadiman, *The Spirit Catches You and You Fall Down*. New York: Noonday, 1997.

Jane Hamilton-Merritt, *Tragic Mountains: The Hmong, the Americans, and the Secret Wars for Laos, 1942-1992*. Bloomington: Indiana University Press, 1999.

Vincent K. Her, *Hmong Mortuary Practices: Self, Place and Meaning in Urban America*. Ann Arbor, MI: ProQuest/ UMI, 2006.

Jo Ann Koltyk and Nancy Foner, *New Pioneers in the Heartland: Hmong Life in Wisconsin*. Boston: Allyn & Bacon, 1997.

Stacey J. Lee, *Learning About Race, Learning About "America": Hmong American High School Students*. Albany: State University of New York Press, 2005.

Fungchatou T. Lo, *The Promised Land: The Socioeconomic Reality of the Hmong People in Urban America (1976-2000)*. Lima, OH: Wyndham Hall, 2001.

Kathleen M. McInnis, Helen E. Petracchi, and Mel Morgenbesser, *The Hmong in America: Providing Ethnic Sensitive Health, Education, and Human Services*. Dubuque, IA: Kendall/Hunt, 1990.

Ines M. Miyarees, *The Hmong Refugees, Experience in the United States: Crossing the River*. Tucson: University of Arizona Press, 1994.

Gayle Morrison, *Sky Is Falling: An Oral History of the CIA's Evacuation of the Hmong from Laos*. Jefferson, NC: McFarland, 1999.

Mai Neng Moua, *Bamboo Among the Oaks: Contemporary Writing by Hmong Americans*. St. Paul, MN: Borealis, 2002.

Naw-Karl Mua, *Hmong Marriage in America: The Paradigm Shift for a Healthy Generation*. Bangkok, Thailand: Prachoomthong, 2002.

Susan Omoto, *Hmong Milestones in America: Citizens in a New World (To Know the Land)*. Evanston, IL: John Gordon Burke, 2003.

Tim Pfaff, *Hmong in America: Journey from a Secret War.* Chippewa Falls, WI: Chippewa Valley Museum, 2005.

Keith Quincy, *Harvesting Pa Chay's Wheat: The Hmong and America's Secret War in Laos.* Spokane: Eastern Washington University Press, 2000.

Keith Quincy, *Hmong.* Spokane: Eastern Washington University Press, 2003.

Takeuchi Shosuke, *Laos as Battlefield.* Tokyo: Mekong, 2005.

Randy Snook, *Many Ideas Open the Way: A Collection of Hmong Proverbs.* Fremont, CA: Shen's, 2003.

Nicholas Tapp and Don Cohn, eds., *The Tribal Peoples of Southeast Asia: Chinese Views of the Other Within.* Bangkok, Thailand: White Lotus, 2003.

Nicholas Tapp, Jean Michaud, Christian Culas, and Gary Yia Lee, eds., *Hmong/Miao in Asia.* Chiang Mai, Thailand: Silkworm, 2004.

Roger Warner, *Shooting at the Moon: The Story of America's Clandestine War in Laos.* Royalton, VT: Steerforth, 1995.

Web Sites

Hmong Cultural Center (www.hmongcenter.org/hmonpop. html). The Hmong Center is a multicultural resource center for Hmong research and cultural understanding. This Web site is full of links to other places of interest on the Web as well as research materials, bibliographies, and cultural exhibits.

Hmong National Development, Inc. (www.hndlink.org). This Web site is home to the Hmong National Development, Inc, an organization committed to build capacity, develop leadership, and empower the Hmong American community. They offer internships, scholarships, economic development advice, and other programs and events designed to help the Hmong community.

The *NEEG* Online (www.neeg.org). The *NEEG* is a magazine for Hmong people in America. This Web site lists news and events as well as interviews and cultural information, in both English and Hmong languages.

Starting Anew, Part II (www.wisinfo.com/legacy/thailand). WisInfo.com, a consortium of Wisconsin news agencies, offers this special report on the Hmong in Wisconsin. It is a good all-around reference on how and why the Hmong arrived in Wisconsin and what their community is doing now.

WWW Hmong Homepage (www.hmongnet.org). This Web site for Hmong information in America features general information, announcements, journals, research documents, and publication reviews.

Index

abuse, 90, 112, 113, 130–34

acculturation. *See* assimilation

Aderholt, Harry (Heinie), 147–50

African Americans, gangs of, 120, 122–23

age, hierarchy of, 108, 111, 114

aging, 56, 61–67

agrarian lifestyle, 20, 48–49, 75, 79

Air America (CIA front company), 120–21, 150

ancestors, 49, 76
    souls of, 64, 66, 71, 73, 76

animals, 49
    sacrifice of, 20, 70, 74, 78, 130

animism, 20, 49

Apocalypse Now (film), 39

Argentina, Hmong in, 36

Asian Americans, 53–54, 156–57
    gangs of, 120, 121–23
    see also Southeast Asians

assimilation, 18–19, 48–54, 69, 76, 80, 102–5
    successes in, 81–91

asylum, application for, 18
    see also citizenship

Australia, Hmong in, 36, 43

authority, lines of, 108, 109

babies, birth of, 163–64

bands, rock, 135–39

Ban Napho (refugee camp), 44, 45

Ban Vinai (refugee camp), 36, 154–55

Bauer, Robert, 68

bee pollen. *See* Yellow Rain

behaviors, changing, 118
    see also culture(s), transition in

beliefs. *See* Hmong, culture of

Bernard, Carl, 39–43, 46

biological warfare, 16, 34, 35, 39

biomedicine, 68, 74–76
    see also medicine, Western

Bloods (gang), 120, 122–23

blood tests, 163

body counts, in Vietnam War, 149
    see also Hmong, killing of

Bonner, Brian, 130

bride wealth, 110–11, 115, 116

businesses, 21–22, 88–90, 92–94, 97–98
    see also entrepreneurs

California, Hmong in, 17, 67, 76, 81–101, 135–39

Cambodia, 41

Canada, 27
    Hmong in, 36

Carter, Jimmy, 45

cell phones, 103–4

Central Intelligence Agency (CIA)
    front companies of, 120–21, 150
    Hmong relationship with, 15, 28–32, 39–40, 43, 45, 141, 151

ceremonies, 72, 75, 78
    see also rituals

charities, 81, 85, 86, 96

Chaudhary, Satveer, 156

chemical warfare, 16, 34, 35, 39

Chiang Kham (refugee camp), 36

children
    abuse of, 130–34
    care of, 55, 56, 59, 61, 67

citizenship for, 53
education of, 50
rejection of parents by, 19, 120, 122, 124–29, 131
roles of, 48, 62–67, 115–16
see also education
China, involvement of, in Laos, 26–28, 40, 42
chiropractors, 75
see also medicine, Western
Christianity
conversion to, 21, 49, 66, 71, 115, 118–19
hatred of, 45
churches, 81, 85, 127–28
Church World Services, 100–101
citizenship, 18, 48, 52–53, 116, 156
City of Refuge (film), 44
clans, 50, 69
disputes handled by, 130–32, 134
marriage into, 64–65, 110, 112
politics of, 142–43
see also patriarchal society
Clinton, Bill, 45
clothing, making of, 22
see also needlework
Colby, William E., 24–32, 145
colleges, 51–52, 82, 99
Communists
fight against, 24, 26, 28, 141–43
hatred of, 45
community, sense of, 105, 128
Connecticut, Hmong in, 99
Coppola, Francis Ford, 39
cost of living, 81, 98
courts. *See* United States, legal system of
Crips (gang), 120, 122–23
culture(s)
clash of, 19, 48, 67, 68–69, 124–34

rejection of, 120, 122
transition in, 15, 26, 75–76, 90, 107–19
see also Hmong, culture of

Dao, Yang, 87
daughters/daughters-in-law, roles of, 65–66, 114
death, rituals for, 21, 163, 164
depression, 76–77, 80, 105
diabetes, 74, 75
Dirks, Suzanne C., 48
disabled persons, 55, 79, 90
discrimination, 14, 126–28, 156
divorce, 107, 111–14, 116
doctors, Western, 71, 73–74
see also medicine, Western
domestic violence, 90, 112, 113, 130–34
Donnelly, Nancy D., 107
drivers education, 67, 90
drug trade, 120, 123

Early Identification Program (EIP), 51–52
Eastern Europe, 37
education, 49–52, 87–88, 104–5, 154
lack of, 22, 48, 56–58, 60
postsecondary, 21–22, 48, 51–54, 82, 99
vocational, 52, 60, 86–87, 96–98
elders, 46, 49–50, 61–67, 90, 124
language barriers for, 48, 52
male, 22, 108, 111, 112, 114
medical care for, 80, 161
employment
barriers to, 55–60
lack of, 51, 95, 96
training for, 52, 60, 86–87, 96–98
see also jobs

English (language)
  limited ability with, 56, 58, 67, 87, 98, 104–5
  study of, 18–19, 51, 85, 88, 91, 116
entrepreneurs, 99–100, 128, 165–68
  see also businesses

families
  abuse in, 130–34
  alienation from, 124–29
  changes in, 107–19
  extended, 49, 61–67, 115
  importance of, 51, 76
  nuclear, 22, 114–15
  size of, 39, 62–63
Fargo, Heather (mayor), 82–83
farming, 64, 65, 66, 92–101, 108
  see also agrarian lifestyle; slash-and-burn farming
fathers, roles of, 116, 133
folk arts, 22, 87, 108–10
food, 128–29
France, Hmong in, 36, 43
French Foreign Legion, 40
French Guyana, Hmong in, 36
French-Indochina War, 39–40, 43

gambling, illegal, 120, 123
gangs, 90, 120–23, 137
gender roles, 22, 49, 52, 64–65, 90, 133–34
  changes in, 107–19
Geneva Accords, 15, 24, 26–30
genocide. *See* Hmong, killing of
Georgia, Hmong in, 98
girls, 50, 130–34
goals, changing, 113, 115, 118
  see also culture(s), transition in
Goetz, Kaomi, 77

government. *See* Minnesota State Legislature; politics; United Nations; United States
grief, 21, 76, 77
group, importance of, 49, 53, 62, 67, 70, 76
guerrilla warfare/warriors, 15, 26, 31, 145
  benefits for, 18, 46
  bravery of, 121, 142, 148–49
  see also resistance movements

Harriman, W. Averell, 29
Harris, Wendy, 161
health, problems with, 55, 56, 64
  see also illnesses; medicine
Helsel, Deborah G., 68
Hiawatha Valley Farm Project, 92, 100–101
Highland Lao Initiative, 92, 96–97, 98, 100
High Voltage (band), 136–37
Hmong
  betrayal of, by U.S., 15–16, 34, 38–46, 52, 121, 126–27, 150
  CIA relationship with, 15, 24–32, 39–40, 43, 45, 51, 141, 145, 151
  culture of, 49–51, 53, 90, 107–10, 112, 117–18, 124, 131, 161, 163–64
  first-generation, in U.S., 14–15, 19–22, 46, 107, 118, 130
  history of, 20, 26, 72
  killing of, 15–17, 21, 26, 31, 33–37, 42, 44–45, 79–80, 149–50
  second-generation, in U.S., 18–19, 21–22, 46, 50, 117, 120–22, 130, 135–39
Hmong (language), 18–19, 129
  lack of written, 48, 50, 52, 58
Hmong/Highlander Development Fund, 95

Hmongmedia Interactive, 165, 167–68

Hmong Men for Peace and Unity, 90

Hmong Special Forces operation, 41–43

Hmong United International Council, 78

Ho Chi Minh trail, 15, 42

hog farming, 93, 94

home ownership, 82, 85, 87, 99

H.R. 371 (bill), 18

H.R. 2202 (bill), 52

hypertension, 74, 75

illnesses
    causes of, 66–67, 68, 69, 74–76
    shamans called through, 70, 71, 73
    traditional treatment of, 20–21, 68–76

immigrants
    first-wave, 14–15, 17–19, 48, 77, 103–5, 166
    second-wave, 102–5
    Vietnamese, 18, 94, 97
    see also refugees

incest, 130–34

income, 82, 98, 107–9, 115
    lack of, 48, 51, 53, 67, 105

India, 27

individualization, 51, 62, 67, 76, 82, 115, 117

Indochina. See French-Indochina War

Indochinese Resource Action Committee, 95

industrialization, 20, 48, 75

International Commission for Supervision and Control of Laos (ICC), 27–28

Iowa, Hmong in, 44

isolation, 67, 76–77, 80, 95, 102–3, 105, 121

Jean, Sheryl, 165

jobs, 86–87, 98–99, 104
    see also employment

Kelly, Randy (mayor), 82, 91

Kennedy, John F., 24, 25, 27, 28, 40

Kennedy, Tony, 141

Khmer Rouge. See Pathet Lao

Killing Fields, 15
    see also Hmong, killing of

kinship, ties of, 110–11
    see also clans; families

Knotts, Jack, 150–52

Korean War, 40

Korpi, Michael, 44, 45

Khrushchev, Nikita, 27

Lair, Bill, 142, 145, 148–50

language barrier, 18–19, 48–50, 53, 55, 67, 105
    see also English (language); Hmong (language)

Laos
    Communist takeover of, 15, 28, 31, 33
    culture of, 14–15, 43, 65, 115
    neutrality of, 27, 30–31
    secret war in, 14–15, 24–32, 40–41, 141
    see also Pathet Lao

Laotian (Language), 19

Latimer, George (mayor), 85

Latin music, 135, 136

Latter Day Saints, Church of, 127–28

Lawrence, Vinton, 146–47, 148

laws, for refugees, 17–18, 52, 53

Lee, Gary Yia, 33
life expectancy, 65
life visas, 68, 69, 71, 72–73
literacy, lack of, 57–58, 60
LoBaido, Anthony C., 38
Loke, Christopher, 124
loneliness. *See* isolation

Magagnini, Stephen, 81
magical spells, 68, 69, 70
marriage, 22, 49, 64–65, 132
    changes in, 107–19, 124–25, 127
    see also domestic violence
McEnroe, Paul, 141
McGarvey, Brendan, 120
medicine
    alternative, 75, 76
    herbal, 69, 74
    Hmong traditional, 20–21, 68–76, 130
    Western, 20, 68, 71–76, 78–79, 161, 163–64
men
    disputes handled by, 130–32, 134
    roles of, 22, 64–65, 107–8, 115–18
    see also elders, male
mental illnesses, 77–80
military-industrial complex, 41–42
Minnesota
    gangs in, 122
    Hmong in, 17, 74, 77–91, 80, 95, 99–105, 130–34, 143, 159, 165–68
Minnesota Hmong Chamber of Commerce, 83
Minnesota State Legislature, 81, 154, 156–57
Missionary Alliance Denomination, 49
mobility, 95–96

Mochel, Marilyn, 68
model minorities, 53–54
money, 49, 115
    see also income
Moore, Thomas, 55
mothers, roles of, 116
Moua, Dang, 92–94
Moua, Mee, 154–57
music/musicians, 135–39

naming ceremonies, 72
naturalization. *See* citizenship
needlework, 22, 87, 108–10
Neo Hom (organization), 143–44
New Year celebrations, 49
New York (state), Hmong in, 99
New Zealand, Hmong in, 43
Nixon, Richard M., 45
nomadic lifestyle, 20, 92
North Carolina, Hmong in, 91, 98–99, 126
North Vietnam, Hmong fight against, 15, 24–31, 34, 42–43, 142, 145, 148–51
    see also Vietname War, Hmong involvement in

opium, 93, 94, 108
organ donations, 163
Oroville Mono Boys (gang), 90

Pao, Vang, 34, 35, 41, 85–86, 141–53
Paradise (band), 135, 136, 137–38
paranoia, 80
parents
    care of, 56, 62–67
    language barriers for, 48
    music for, 137, 138
    rejection of, by children, 19, 120, 122, 124–29, 131
    roles of, 116, 133

Pathet Lao
    Hmong fight against, 28, 33–37, 46, 52, 141–43, 151
    killing of Hmong by, 15–17, 34–37, 39, 44–46, 102
patriarchal society, 22, 48–49, 65–66, 133
    see also clans; men
Pennsylvania, Hmong in, 120–23
Phanat Nikhom (refugee camp), 36
pickle farms, 97–98
Planned Secondary Resettlement Project, 98–99
Poland, 27
politics, 21–22, 156–57
polygamy, 49, 115
population control, 39
poverty, 50, 76, 87, 121
prejudice, 14, 126–28, 156, 159
Project Respectism, 158, 159–60
prostitution, 120, 123
Protestantism, 115
    see also Christianity
psychiatry, rejection of, 77–80
    see also medicine, Western
public assistance. *See* welfare programs

racism, 14, 126–28, 156, 159
Randolph, Toni, 102
Refugee Act (1980), 17–18
refugee camps, 16–19, 33–36, 43–45, 103–4, 121–22
refugees
    life as, 26, 31, 33–37, 52, 66
    resettlement of, 17, 81
    see also immigrants
relief funds, 18
    see also welfare programs
religion, 20–21, 49, 77, 118–19
    see also Christianity; churches
renal failure, 75

repatriation, 16–17, 36–39, 43–46
resettlement, 81, 84, 94–99, 104
resettlement villages. *See* seminar centers
resistance movements, 33–37, 46, 52
respect, 48, 108
Rhode Island, Hmong in, 99
rituals, 20–21, 64, 68–69, 74–75, 110
    see also ceremonies
role models, 52
Russia. *See* Soviet Union

S. 1664 (bill), 53
sacrifices. *See* animals, sacrifice of
Sayaovong, Amoun Vang, 24
schools, 87–88, 99, 124
    see also education
self-sufficiency. *See* individualization
Selkowe, Vicky, 55
seminar centers, 33, 34, 36–37
shamans, 20–21, 68–80, 130
Sherman, Spencer, 92
skills, lack of, 20, 48, 55–58, 93–94, 103–4, 108
    see also education, vocational
slash-and-burn farming, 20, 49, 92, 93–94
social services, 81, 85, 86, 96
social structures, changes in, 63–64, 75–76, 90, 107–19
    see also culture(s), transition in
sons, roles of, 64–66
souls
    of ancestors, 64, 73
    search for, 70–72
    shamans' work with, 68, 69, 70–72, 164
    theory of, 20, 115, 163–64
soul-splitting ceremonies, 72

Southeast Asians, 18, 24–26, 52, 74–75

  see also individual countries

Soviet Union, 15, 16, 37

  involvement of, in Laos, 26–28, 42

spirits, 64, 73, 75, 77–79, 130, 142, 146

  illnesses caused by, 20–21, 69–71, 76, 77–79, 164

State of Minnesota vs. Za Xiong, 130–34

statistics

  on deaths of Hmong in Laos, 15, 31, 33, 35, 42, 79–80

  on education, 51–52, 53

  on elderly population, 66

  on Hmong population in U.S., 17–18, 21, 43, 50, 81–82, 96, 102, 132

  on refugee resettlement, 35–36, 43

stress, illnesses caused by, 21, 75–76, 79–80

Sullivan, William, 24, 29–30

supernatural events, illness caused by, 68, 69

technology, 103–4, 165

  lack of experience with, 19, 79

Teng, Ly, 146, 150

Texas, Hmong in, 98–99

Thailand, Hmong refugees in, 82, 91, 102, 141, 154–55

  see also refugee camps

tonal languages, 18–19, 129

traditions, 20, 90, 161

  rejection of, 19, 124–29

  see also culture(s)

transition. *See* assimilation; culture(s), transition in

transportation, lack of, 55, 56, 67

trauma. *See* stress, illnesses caused by

tribes. *See* clans

United Bamboo Triad (gang), 120, 123

United Front for the Liberation of Laos, 35

  see also resistance movements

United Nations, 45

  Children's Fund (UNICEF), 39

  High Commission for Refugees (UNHCR), 17, 36, 38, 44, 154

United States

  betrayal of Hmong by, 15–16, 34, 38–46, 52, 121, 126–27, 150

  culture of, 14–15, 19, 124

  Department of State, 39, 45

  legal system of, 112, 113, 115, 130–34

  Office of Refugee Resettlement, 17, 96, 98

  population of Hmong in, 17–18, 21, 43, 50, 81–82, 96, 102, 132

  secret wars of, 14–15, 24–32, 120–21, 141–42

  in Vietnam War, 14–16, 38–46, 126–27

  see also Central Intelligence Agency; laws, for refugees

Utah, Hmong in, 126–29

values, changing, 18

  see also culture(s), transition in

Vang, Cha, 84

Vang, Chai, 14

Vang, Yer, 97–98

Vang Pao Foundation, 144

Viet Cong, 40, 42–43
  see also North Vietnam,
    Hmong fight against
Vietnamese (language), 19
Vietnamese Americans, 18, 94, 97,
  122
Vietnam War, 24–26, 149
  end of, 33, 38
  Hmong involvement in, 14–
    16, 39–42, 77, 80, 126–28
  see also North Vietnam,
    Hmong fight against
violence, 14, 79, 143
  see also domestic violence;
    gangs
VTK (gang), 122
Vue, Na Vongsa, 124–29

Washington (state), Hmong in, 32,
  108, 114
wealth, 49
  see also bride wealth; income
weddings, 107, 110–11, 117
welfare programs, 50, 55, 86, 90,
  96–99

Whyteshadows (band), 136, 138
Wisconsin
  gangs in, 122
  Hmong in, 17, 50–52, 55–60,
    95–98, 155–64
wives, 115, 117
women
  advancement of, 22, 87, 90,
    107–19
  roles of, 49, 52, 64–65, 115–
    18, 133–34

Xiong, Nzong, 135, 158
Xiong, Tou Ger, 84, 88, 158–60
Xiong, Xa, 161–64
Xiong, Za, 130–33

Yang, Bill, 165–68
Yang, Fong, 166–67
Yang, Kao-Ly, 61
Yarborough, William P., 42
Yellow Rain, 16
youth, 46, 50, 53–54, 90, 107–39